# PSYCHOPATHS

and

# SOCIOPATHS

and

# ANTISOCIAL BEHAVIOR

I0421366

# ARE YOU ONE?

BY

# Dr. Gerald A. Walford

# ACKNOWLEDGEMENTS

CLAUDE L. CRUM Ph.D. was instrumental in editing this book. His experience as an English Professor and College Dean was most helpful in the organization of book as well as the grammar and syntax.

*PUBLISHED BOOKS by Dr. Gerald A. Walford*

Biography:
CONTROLLING ADVERSITY.

Baseball/softball:
THE BASEBALL/SOFTBALL SWING OF THE FUTURE.

Concentration:
CONCENTRATION AND OTHER MENTAL SKILLS FOR
SPORTS, LIFE AND THE ARTS.

E-books amazon:
HOW TO WRITE A BOOK.
KARATE CHOP GOLF.

Golf: (Class A - Professional Golfers' Association of
America). THE GOLF SUPERBOOK (700 page book).
 SLAPSHOT GOLF - learning golf through the hockey
slapshot and baseball swing.
THE GOLF WHISPERER.
PERFORMANCE GOLF.
GOLF'S POWER SECRETS.
PRACTICAL GOLF COACHING MANUAL for the World
Golf Teachers Federation.

History:
SPORT, RELIGION AND WAR – Through the Ages

Hockey:

---

COACHING GIRLS ICE HOCKEY.
COACHING HOCKEY.
HOCKEY SKILLS.
YOUTH HOCKEY.
ICE HOCKEY - AN ILLUSTRATED GUIDE.

Humor: Major area of Ph.D. study.
HUMOR AND PERSONALITY.
SPORT HUMOR.

Humor, Psychology And Medical:
I MAY BE CRAZY BUT I AM NOT STUPID – The Life of a Mental Patient on the PGA Tour

leadership:
DETERMINING THE FUTURE THROUGH LEADERSHIP SKILLS.

Mystery Novel:
THE LADY SPY AND CON MAN

Psychology:
PSYCHOPATHS  and SOCIOPATHS and ANTISOCIAL BEHAVIOR

Teaching:
THE TAO OF TEACHING.

# TABLE OF CONTENTS

**PART TWO:** PSYCHOPATHS WHO KILL

# BIBLIOGRAPHY

# DEFINITIONS

Psychopathy = mental illness

From psyche – mind, and pathos, disease

Psychopaths are often inappropriately labeled as "crazy" or "psycho" but the terms are not fully accurate as psychopaths know what they are doing and why they do it. Society does not necessarily agree with them.

Psychopathy is a syndrome – a group of related symptoms and traits that are mostly genetic.

Sociopathy is a syndrome of related symptoms and traits that result from the environment. Non-psychopaths often have some of the symptoms of sociopathy.

Antisocial behavior is often the term used for a psychopathic or a sociopathic person.

Although the terms and names for each syndrome are different, the symptoms are very similar. Even psychologists and psychiatrists often use the terms interchangeably.

# CHAPTER ONE

# Dr. ROBERT HARE

Dr. Robert Hare has studied and researched psychopathy for more than forty years while at the University of British Columbia, in Canada. He has written many books and articles on the subject of psychopathy but his main contribution to the field is his PSYCHOPATHY CHECKLIST-REVISED (PCL-R). The PCL-R has also been altered for adaptation to other specific areas like for youth, law enforcement, antisocial behaviors, etc.

His work with the FBI (Federal Bureau of Investigation) and RCMP (Royal Canadian Mounted Police) and other international agencies has earned him many highest awards from nations throughout the world.

When we think of psychopaths, we usually think in terms of murder, violence, rape, and other atrocious crimes. Some psychopaths are not necessarily of this violent nature as Hare points out in his book SNAKES IN SUITS: WHEN PSYCHOPATHS GO TO WORK.

Psychopaths are also in the business world, home, next door neighbors, coaching and sports world. Looking at the PCL-R test we can see how this is possible. Buros

Mental Measurements Yearbook (1995) claimed that the PCL-R was state of the art for clinical and research use. In 2005, they claimed the PCL-R is the gold standard for measurement of psychopathy. The PCL-R is adopted worldwide.

He has consulted with law enforcement, including the FBI and the RCMP, was a member of the former Research Advisory Board of the FBI Child Abduction and Serial Murder Investigative Resources Center (CASMIRC), and is an Affiliate Member of the International Criminal Investigative Analysis Fellowship. He also was a member of the Advisory Panel established by Her Majesty's Prison Service to develop new programs for the treatment of psychopathic offenders.

His current research on psychopathy includes assessment issues, developmental factors, neurobiological correlates, risk for recidivism and violence, and the development (with S. Wong) of new treatment and management strategies for psychopathic offenders (Guidelines for a Psychopathy Treatment Program).

He and Paul Babiak have extended the theory and research on psychopathy to the business and corporate world, with the development of the B-Scan-360, a 360° instrument used to screen for psychopathic traits and behaviors, and a book, SNAKES IN SUITS:

WHEN PSYCHOPATHS GO TO WORK. He lectures widely on psychopathy and on the use and misuse of the PCL-R in the mental health and criminal justice systems.

Among his most recent awards are the Silver Medal of the Queen Sophia Center in Spain.

The Canadian Psychological Association Award for Distinguished Applications of Psychology.

The American Academy of Forensic Psychology Award for Distinguished Applications to the Field of Forensic Psychology.

The Isaac Ray Award presented by the American Psychiatric Association and the American Academy of Psychiatry and Law for Outstanding Contributions to Forensic Psychiatry and Psychiatric Jurisprudence.

The B. Jaye Anno Award for Excellence in Communication, presented by the National Commission on Correctional Health Care.

The Lifetime Achievement Award presented by the Society for the Scientific Study of Psychopathy.

The CPA Award for Distinguished Contributions to the International Advancement of Psychology.

The CPA Donald O. Hebb Award for Distinguished Contributions to Psychology as a Science.

the Western Society of Criminology's Paul Tappan Award for Outstanding Contributions to the Field of Criminology.

The British Columbia Psychological Association's Award for Recognition of a Distinguished Career and Enduring Contributions to Psychology.

The Order of Canada presented by the Governor General of Canada recognizing a lifetime of outstanding achievement, dedication to community and service to the nation; and from the Center for the Advancement of Psychological Science and Law, recognition for Distinguished Lifetime Achievements as a Leader in Psychology and Law, and Outstanding Contributions to Forensic Psychology.

Robert Hare says that back in the 1960's, it was thought criminals were made not born. Until the present, there was very little research on psychopaths. Environmental factors were considered crime factors as you were born with a clean slate and could be trained to be anything.

Dr. Hare could not buy into this belief as he thought inborn personality was important as there were just too many differences in people. We all have individual differences in intelligence so why not individual differences in personality traits in how people relate to crime, violence, empathy and feelings of guilt?

Hare started to study, research and experiment with criminals at the nearby prison looking for personality traits that may lead to criminology.

In an experimental electric shock study, he told the inmates that in 30 seconds he was going to shock them with an intense electric shock. He measured their heart rates to see if this information of the shock would bother them. Most of the prisoners were bothered, but a few were not.

What was interesting was that most people will show emotional arousal, anticipation fear, and anxiety in waiting for the shock. This is a normal reaction, but the few who showed no reactions were labeled psychopaths. They had no emotions.

Later, researchers found that no emotions were shown in the amygdala of the brain. The amygdala registers fear, but for some reason it does not work in the brains of the psychopaths.

Another interesting experiment found that psychopaths when startled, while being absorbed in something, usually do not respond like normal people by jumping or being greatly startled or surprised.

In another test, Hare showed prisoners emotional pictures like rape, killings, violence, etc. and neutral pictures like a table, chair, etc. The violent pictures would create a response from most of the prisoners but the psychopaths showed no reaction. Psychopaths showed a neutral reaction to all pictures.

Hare concluded that psychopathic personalities were emotionally deaf, with no capacity to feel emotions like empathy, love, remorse, guilt, etc.

At the time, there was no reliable, clear or standard way to identify or measure who was or was not a psychopath. A measurement tool was needed and so he created the PCL-R.

With his assistant, they compiled a list of every personality trait they found in their studies. They came up with 20 traits with a scoring system of "0" points if the trait did not apply, "1" point if the psychologist could not tell for sure but possible and "2" points if the trait was there. A perfect score was 40 but anything over 30 certified the test taker as a psychopath.

The test listed 20 traits to check, and so Hare called it the Psychopath Checklist (PCL). Scores were totaled at the end — 40 was the highest score, but anything over 30 certified the test taker as a psychopath.

Reliability tests were astonishingly good. The test became the standard around the world.

(http://www.npr.org/2011/05/26/136619689/can-a-test-really-tell-whos-a-psychopath).

Basically the test is designed to rate behavior (antisocial or psychopathy) with an objective score rather than a subjective score. An example of objective score would be like in a hockey game 3 to 2, or in golf 78 score. The evaluation is precise and accurate. No debate on the score. A subjective score would be like in gymnastics or figure skating where the score comes from the opinions of the judges.

In the mid 1980's, Randy Kropp, a student of Hare's, used the test to determine how the criminals and psychopaths faired after their release from prison. He arranged the prisoners into groups of high, medium and low scores to see how the scores compared to their likelihood of committing crimes after their release from prison and on parole.

About 20 to 25 percent of those that scored low on the PCL-R (PSYCHOPATH CHECKLIST – REVISED) would be re-convicted while 80 percent of the high scores were convicted within four or five years.

These percentages helped to verify the legitimacy of the PCL-R test in identifying the psychopath and helping to determine the future of criminals.

Naturally, the psychological world was stunned as the new PCL-R research challenged the old ideas and beliefs that criminal behavior was learned or resulted from environmental factors (nurture). The PCL- R now brings in the genetic factors (nature). Now, the nature overrides nurture?

Hare was reluctant to release the test as he felt it had the potential for misuse in untrained hands. He wanted only scientists and psychologists to have access. Demands were too great, so he relented and it went public.

Controversy on the test did occur as Hare predicted. Test administrators must be highly trained. Personal biases can easily taint the score.

Daniel Murrie, a University of Virginia professor, says things often change when psychological tests are taken from the research environment and applied to the criminal world.

Murrie compared the PCL-R scores by psychologists hired by the prosecution with the scores by psychologists hired by the defense. He found that the scores did not agree with an average of an eight point difference. Murrie feels that it is possible that the testers were not well trained. (Sometimes there is too much adherence to the exact score when some fluctuation should be considered. It would be like score of 78 for a C grade while a score of 81 for a B grade does not real signify one as really that much smarter than the other).

Murrie also points out an interesting result in that the scores from the prosecution consistently had higher scores than the scores from the defense. A little bias here? Perhaps it is the money bias as to who pays the tester?

Psychopaths are manipulative, in acting like they care and have empathy. This is one of the traits that makes scoring difficult. Testers must be able to recognize these manipulative tendencies.

It is natural that Hare is upset by this use of the test by some people so he travels the country and world to train test administrators.

> I'm very concerned about the inappropriate use of this instrument for purposes that have serious implications for individuals and for society. It shouldn't work that way.

The PCL-R is still used by many in law enforcement. It is even mandated by statute in several states. Once again the proper training is required. The test is still a good guideline and it must be used as a guideline. Careless administration can give someone a label that cannot be rescinded. A mistake in scoring can put someone away for life.

Alix Spiegel of the ALL THINGS CONSIDERED program on NPR radio had a panel discussion on the PCL-R test. The following are comments by the three panelists.

Karen Franklin on Masking Bias with Science

Karen Franklin is a clinical and forensic psychologist in the San Francisco Bay Area and an adjunct professor at the California School of Professional Psychology.

Her title of masking bias with science covers her opinion quite well. To her, evaluation is very subjective and bias can affect the outcome. An objective score does not give the full picture, as such a score can be used for labeling. Objective scores have a powerful effect on judges and jurors as an objective score seems so final and yet so easy to understand and interpret.

(http://www.npr.org/2011/05/26/136433233/expert-panel-weighing-the-value-of-a-test-for-psychopaths?tab=2).

Henry Richards, Ph.D. on Identifying the Bad Apples

Richards is forensic psychologist in private practice and was formerly an executive overseeing statewide treatment programs for offenders in Maryland and Washington state. Richards is an associate clinical professor at the University of Washington School of Medicine and an associate professor of criminal justice at Seattle University.

Henry Richards claims the PCL-R is a reliable tool in identifying pathologic offenders. The test also helps in determining treatment and intervention strategies.

Despite their destructive and repetitive conduct, many psychopaths are good at making excuses to trained professionals, eliciting sympathy and even admiration for their intrepid resolve to reform themselves. This makes subjective evaluation difficult.

Test scores can also help predict how someone might perform on conditional release like bail, probation, or parole. PCL-R scores can help guide choices about the type of institutional or community supervision that may be needed for the rehabilitation of the inmate.

(http://www.npr.org/2011/05/26/136433233/expert-panel-weighing-the-value-of-a-test-for-psychopaths?tab=3)


John Edens, Ph.D. Unreliable and Stigmatizing Tool

John Edens, Ph.D., is a licensed psychologist and professor of psychology at Texas A&M University. He has published an array of research articles on psychopathy and forensic psychology and is identified in Thompson Scientific's "Essential Science Indicators" as in the top 1 percent of cited researchers in the psychology/psychiatry field over the past 10 years. He currently serves on the editorial board of numerous scientific journals (e.g., PSYCHOLOGICAL ASSESSMENT, LAW & HUMAN BEHAVIOR) and is a former associate editor of the scientific journal ASSESSMENT.

Edens feels the test may have value in certain circumstances but care must be taken in overestimation of the score. He claims many people who do not have psychopathic personalities have extensive criminal histories. He does agree that the personality component of the PCL-R is important when determining how dangerous a person is. The personality component evaluates such things as a lack of remorse or guilt, appears callous, seems superficially charming, and has an inflated sense of self-worth. Some experts disagree on the personality component of the PCL-R, perhaps because scoring it involves much more subjective judgment than does the criminal history component.

(http://www.npr.org/2011/05/26/136433233/expert-panel-weighing-the-value-of-a-test-for-psychopaths?tab=4).

http://www.npr.org/2011/05/26/136619689/can-a-test-really-tell-whos-a-psychopath

# CHAPTER TWO

# THE PSYCHOPATHY CHECKLIST - REVISED TEST

Scoring the test:

0 points if it does not apply.

1 point if it applies partially

2 points it applies.

The score for clinical pathology is around 30 and above.

As you go through the test you will notice how some of the factors interrelate with each other.

## 1. Glib and Superficial Charm
Psychopathic charm is evident in being smooth, charming, slick, engaging, with easy verbal skills, not in the least bit shy or self-conscious. They are willing to speak out on anything. They rarely get tongue-tied or at a loss for words.

## 2. Grandiose Sense of Self-Worth
Psychopaths believe they are superior to all. Naturally, this is exemplified in the over-rated belief in their self-worth, and self-assuredness. They are never wrong.

They are the supreme authority. They are cocky and brag excessively. They are arrogant.

## 3. Need for stimulation and a Proneness to Boredom

Psychopaths are risk seekers. They need stimulation and excitement. This may well be why some kill and/or become serial killers. The Zodiac killer in San Francisco killed and taunted the police with clues for his excitement. Psychopaths are usually low in self-discipline. They often fail to complete tasks as the tasks get boring, and the excitement dies.

## 4. Pathological Lying

They can be shrewd, crafty, cunning, sly, clever, deceptive, underhanded, unscrupulous, manipulative and dishonest. They are very deceitful. Their behavior is used to protect their self-image, ego and self-worth.

## 5. Conning and Manipulative

This coincides with number 4 as to being deceitful, cheating, conning others, all for personal gain. Number 5 is just a little more ruthless in their exploitation of others as shown in their lack of concern for the feelings and sufferings of their victims.

## 6. Lack of Remorse or Guilt

The suffering and pain of victims is of no concern to psychopaths as suffering and pain is the victim's problem as they feel that the victim deserved it. They lack empathy. They are dispassionate and coldhearted. Their only concern is themselves.

## 7. Shallow Affect
They have emotional poverty, with a limited range or depth of feelings. They can show open gregariousness but it is an act.

## 8. Callousness and Lack of Empathy
Their behavior in being cold, contemptuous, inconsiderate and tactless shows in their lack of feelings for others.

## 9. Parasitic Lifestyle
Their lack of motivation and selfishness puts them in position to exploit others for financial dependence and gain. They have a feeling of deserving what they want.

## 10. Poor Behavioral Controls
Inadequate control of anger and temper is a common behavior. They act hastily with little or no thought of outcome. They easily express irritability, annoyance, impatience, threats, aggression and verbal abuse to others.

## 11. Promiscuous Sexual Behavior

Sexual behavior adds to their need for excitement and for material for bragging about their sexual conquests and affairs. The more affairs, partners, varied partners, and offbeat relationships the more material they have to brag about. Their partners do not last long.

## 12. Early Behavior Problems
Behavior prior to age 13 is filled with lying, theft, cheating, vandalism, bullying, sexual activity, arson, glue sniffing, alcohol use, and often running away from home.

## 13. Lack of Realistic, Long-Term Goals
Psychopaths fail to develop long term goals. A lack of motivation, interest and stimulation causes this as they are concerned with the present only. Their life is aimless, nomadic and lacking in direction.

## 14. Impulsivity
Like number 13 their attitude shows a lack of planning with no thought as to the consequences of their actions. Temptations, frustrations, urges, rashness, recklessness erratic and unpredictable behavior plague the psychopath.

## 15. Irresponsibility
Irresponsibility shows up in failure to pay bills, loans, and honoring obligations and commitments. In the

work place they do sloppy work and are often late or even fail to show up. Like in their failure to pay bills they fail to honor contractual agreements as they feel they deserve in not having to pay.

## 16. Failure to Accept Responsibility for Own Actions

Everything is someone else's fault. It is never them, as they are superior humans and so they have no faults. This leads them to low conscientiousness, an absence of dutifulness, antagonistic manipulation, denial of responsibility, and an effort to manipulate others through this denial.

## 17. Many Short-Term Marital Relationships

This is natural as long-term relationships are not everyday excitement. They get bored easily for more sexual stimulation outside marriage. Marriage is commitment and commitment is not in their personality.

## 18. Juvenile Delinquency

This is self-explanatory. Between the ages of 13 and 18 they have crimes involving aspects of antagonism, exploitation, aggression, manipulation, or a callous, ruthless tough-mindedness. This is similar to number 12.

## 19. Revocation of Condition Release

A revocation of probation or other conditional release due to technical violations, such as carelessness, low deliberation, or failing to appear. This is a failure to live up to their conditions of release.

## 20. Criminal Versatility
They take great pride in their criminal behavior, especially about the crimes they got away with. Their bragging is to show their superiority over the law and society.

# CHAPTER THREE

## OTHER PSYCHOPATH TESTS

There are other psychopath tests but none are as valid or reliable as the PCL-R. Some tests have many of the same questions. Some have almost the same questions and some are just social party games.

The following are a few samples of other psychopath tests.

The PSYCHOPATH TEST by Vistriai is their own creation and is based on the Hare Psychopath Checklist (PCL), before the revision. It is not a replacement to any professional test of psychopathy as it is not clinically administered. Instead, it is only offered for educational purposes, to help people learn about                                     psychopathy. (http://vistriai.com/psychopathtest).

If you take the test you will notice the questions are similar to the PCL-R test but require a simple yes or no. There is no subjective reasoning as in the PCL-R test. It is quick, easy and fun. If you go to the web site you can take the test and receive a score but they do not tell you how the score is counted. But it is interesting.

Because the PCL may be ambiguous to non-trained people this test is designed for easy understanding with simple yes or no answers.

Here is an interesting psychopath test that involves only one answer.

This is a psychological test. It is a story about a girl. While at a funeral of her own mother, she met a guy whom she did not know. (http://www.snopes.com/inboxes/hoaxes/sister.asp).

She thought the guy was amazing, so much her dream guy she believed him to be, that she fell in love with him there and then. . . A few days later, the girl killed her sister?

Question: what was her motive for killing her sister?

The answer is in the next paragraph.

If you answered this correctly, you think like a psychopath. This test was a test by a famous American psychologist to test if one has the same mentality as a killer. Many arrested serial killers took part in this test and answered it correctly. If you didn't answer correctly - good for you. The correct answer is that she was hoping the guy would appear at the funeral.

The above quiz is added here to show you how the internet can be used to deceive and distort into making people possibly believe it is a valid test. The first critical analysis should be in the "test by a famous American psychologist." In truth, the name of the famous American psychologist would have been stated. Although a fictitious name could have been used at least the name could be checked out.

Psychological test have a name and this test has no name.

It must be known that psychopaths are not necessarily stupid. In the story the girl is so smitten by the man she should have perhaps introduced herself or found a way to talk to him. But, then again some people when they see a celebrity or famous person they can easily freeze and do nothing and regret it later on and hope to rectify it some other time.

Can one question or story actually determine one's mental capacity? Psychological tests are often multi questions. The Minnesota Multiphasic Personality Inventory (MMPI) in its original form had 567 items but has been scaled down to 338. This test is considered the gold standard in personality testing. The test is used to identify personality structure and psychopathology. Federal agencies use the test to evaluate top secret security clearances.

Determining psychological problems is not easy. When a psychopath or sociopath kills we think they all are killers, but this is not necessarily so. Many are law-abiding people appearing normal but who just do not know right from wrong shows a lack of care or concern of others and other characteristics that we have seen in the PCL-R. They are out there and many of them are leaders in society. The reason some do not kill is that the consequences of killing are just too great so they stay within the law.

HOW TO SPOT A PSYCHOPATH
By Robert Matthews in the Sunday Telegraph
Review, May 4, 1997.
(http://www.cix.co.uk/~klockstone/teleg.htm).

Do they have problems sustaining stable relationships, personally and in business?

Do they frequently manipulate others to achieve selfish goals, with no consideration of the effects on those manipulated?

Are they cavalier about the truth, and capable of telling lies to your face?

Do they have an air of self-importance, regardless of their true standing in society?

Have they no apparent sense of remorse, shame or guilt?

Is their charm superficial, and capable of being switched on to suit immediate ends?

Are they easily bored and demand constant stimulation?

Are their displays of human emotion unconvincing?

Do they enjoy taking risks, and acting on reckless impulse?

Are they quick to blame others for their mistakes?

As teenagers, did they resent authority, play truant and/or steal?

Do they have no qualms about sponging off others?

Are they quick to lose their temper?

Are they sexually promiscuous?

Do they have a belligerent, bullying manner?

Are they unrealistic about their long-term aims?

Do they lack any ability to empathize with others?

A score of 25 or above suggests strong psychopathic tendencies. This does not mean the person is a potential mass-murderer: socialized psychopaths are not mad, nor do they have to resort to violence. Even so, a close professional or emotional relationship with a socialized psychopath is likely to prove a damaging experience.

# CHAPTER FOUR
# NON-KILLING PSYCHOPATHS

Early in the nineteenth century, Phillip Pinel, a French psychiatrist, claimed that there is a madness that did not involve mania, depression or psychosis. He called it insanity without delusions, "manie sans delire". He said that sufferers appeared normal but lacked impulse controls and were prone to outbursts of violence.

Pinel was ahead of his time. People considered insane were locked up and almost forgotten. He was instrumental in the development of a more humane treatment of mental patients for what was termed "moral therapy." Some consider him the "the father of modern psychiatry." He divorced himself from the religious aspect in mental problems. Back then, religion, God and the Devil were responsible for mental illness and insanity.

Later in 1891 a German doctor, J.L.A. Koch gave it the name psychopathy in his book Die Psychopatischen Minderwertigkeiter.

(http://www.fraud-magazine.com/article.aspx?id=404)

The research by Dr. Hare has shown us that the great majority of psychopaths are not violent criminals.

Many psychopaths live and work with us. They can be anybody from a parent, friend, lover, boss, celebrity, or politician. These people are called "subclinical psychopaths" as they create pain and problems with the people they associate with and they have no remorse or empathy about it.

Fraudulent behavior is common in society. The little white lie or the fib is often associated with this type of behavior. But at this level it is a minor problem as sometimes the fib does prevent a large scale problem. For example, the wife asks her husband if this dress makes me look fat. A simple but loaded question. The husband's reply had better be 'no' even though she would expect that answer from him. So the compliment is lightly taken. However the law of infidelity may prevail later when a stranger tells the wife the dress makes her look sexy and slim. A compliment by a stranger means more than a compliment by a significant other, and psychopaths know this. It is part of their glib, choice of words and ability to manipulate people. Using the law of infidelity we know what the stranger, a psychopath, is after as it works for his sexual promiscuity.

Unfortunately, this introduction may lead to an affair that may lead to losses in financial wealth, property, and even emotional stability of the victim because of the scam by the psychopath. Sometimes death has been involved.

Often with the psychopath, the lies escalate, the behavior becomes manipulative, deceptive, cheating, etc. When lacking remorse or empathy towards a victim these traits are natural to psychopaths as they feel they are entitled to their desires. Victims are to be exploited for their benefit as the victim deserved such actions, the victims should know better, "who cares".

These white collar psychopaths are often involved in embezzlement and pilfering from petty cash. Sometimes the scams are well into the millions of dollars. Because of the lack of physical harm or murder the crimes often get light sentences. Hide the money, receive the light sentence, and live it up on release from prison.

With incidents like the above Drs. Paul Babiak and Robert Hare developed the B-Scan to determine dysfunctional behavior in organizations. Their research of over 200 senior managers, executives, CEO's, etc. led to categorized areas of problematic behaviors:

Personal Style. How individuals see themselves and how they feel about others.

Emotional Style. An understanding of their own feelings and feelings of others (empathy).

Organizational effectiveness. A feeling for what it takes to be a contributing member of an organization or team.

Social responsibility. How effective an individual is in interacting with others.

They came up with over 100 items relevant to business personnel that caused problems in the work force. Such problems would need training, coaching and intervention strategies for correction.

As we look at these four categories we can see how many of the areas are also in line with the Psychological Checklist - Revised test. Empathy, concern for others, feelings, are all associated with psychopaths at a higher level.

When diagnosing a psychopath, we must not let one factor be a determinant or override other factors. A diagnosis must entail the sequence of traits often interacting with each other. Sometimes a glib talker is just a glib talker. Sometimes a symptom does not a disease make. As Sigmund Freud said "sometimes a cigar is just a cigar".

When analyzing the items of personality disorders there is no clear cut score to determine normalcy and psychopathy. It is much like a blood pressure test. The higher the score goes the higher the chance for hypertension and risk to health. It is the range that the score falls in that determines the chance of psychopathy. In many cases, the concern in the diagnosis is the safety and rights of others.

Some people may be just difficult to live, work and play with and are not psychopaths or sociopaths but are the proverbial "pain in the ass."

The common question is what does the psychopath want? In many ways, it is just what the normal person wants, power, prestige, wealth, love, and respect, but these desires are taken to the extreme with the psychopath. They feel they are entitled to these desires and will hurt anyone to obtain them since they have no empathy or concern for other's feelings. Their concern is themselves - only. After all, they are shallow, often display anger, hostility, and frustration due to their lack of empathy, love, shame and sorrow for others. If needed they can act out these emotions but it is an act and not a real feeling. They act it out to hide their true lack of feelings so as not to disclose their true emotions.

An interesting concern is that if psychopaths have no empathy how can they know it in others or know when to use it. They actually learn it through body language and verbal comments from others. They learn to read people. They are observant in others. In many ways the psychopath is a lay psychologist and often very good at it.

Robert Hare claims that psychopaths know the words but not the music. They know the words to use but do not feel the meanings. They can say, "I love you", or "I'm sorry" but it is just a saying with no real feeling or emotions.

There are confusing labels between a psychopath and a sociopath. Basically the terms are used interchangeably by psychologists and behavioral scientists. A sociopath is often the result of environmental factors like upbringing. Psychopaths are the result of psychological traits. The terms are interchangeable because each is influenced by the other.

If we look at the basic structure we see that psychology is the study of the individual's personality and behavior. Sociology is the study of the group. When the individual is influenced by the group it is peer pressure and when the individual influences the group it is called leadership. Peer pressure and leadership can be good or bad, either way the definitions stand.

In many ways the female and male psychopath are similar in egocentricity, deceptiveness, shallow emotions and lack of empathy. In the business world this often shows up with the women leaders. The big difference is that the women are evaluated more harshly than the men when showing these traits.

Psychopaths have great verbal skills, an air of confidence and likeability when being interviewed. These skills often get them the job. The person doing the interview has to be trained in analyzing the answers of the applicant for deception and lying. Research has shown that many applications for job positions have lies, exaggerations and half-truths. And this is not just by the psychopaths.

The resumes of applicants must be thoroughly checked before the interview. It is also a good idea to have various people at different levels of management interview the applicant so that their stories match and show no inconsistencies at each interview. Using many interviewers will make it a little more difficult for the applicant to manipulate one interviewer.

Psychopaths in business and other organizations seek out possible targets that can possibly help them. Such targets are not just their bosses but everyone. Secretaries with their access to much information are excellent targets. Psychopaths use charm and seductive techniques and if necessary blackmail is used. It must be remembered that they will go to any extreme to get what they want.

Psychopaths are always on stage as they see themselves as the directors, writers, produces and as the star actors in their drama of life. Their associates in the organization are nothing but pawns, or simply bit part actors, to support the psychopath in their desires.

The psychopath will form bonds with some of these pawns, but it is not a real bond, as it is just means to an end of getting to where they want to go. With this bond, the psychopath will use and manipulate the pawn. Once this pawn is no longer useful, the bond is severed as the bond has served its purpose. Identifying the target, manipulating the target and then abandoning the target are consistent patterns of the psychopath. The abandonment phase can be a deadly, or a severe problem as hostility can easily be created.

Top management is often not the real leaders. The real leaders are the people who get things done that make the top management look good. The psychopaths pick these people as their targets as they have the real power.

Within the organization it is difficult to pick out the psychopaths as even psychologists are often fooled by their charm and deception. One should look for inconsistencies in behavior and conflicting statements, especially about the past. It is easy to say this but be wary of too much interest in the beginning of meeting.

Perhaps they are coming on too strong with too much superlatives in their compliments. If in doubt, ease back. Also, one should look at their position in the group, their power in the group and what they have that would be of interest and also needed by such a person.

Since psychopaths are only for themselves they are usually loners but they will team up with someone, another psychopath, if their personal gain can be increased. This teaming up usually does not last too long because it is hard with two psychopaths each demanding center stage. Psychopaths do not like to be told what to do or even reaching an agreement with another. They want to do it their way as their ego says they are the best and they are always right.

Anything that can be used to a psychopath's advantage will be used. The internet has been a big boon as it is so easy to contact people. Type your message and just send to all, hundreds of people or even thousands of people, with just the one click. Scams, phony stocks, investments, and identity theft are rampant on the internet. We have familiar scams of "You have been tracked as an heir to the ___ fortune and if you send us the following information we will deposit the 4 million into your account. How about this one "we have 5 million that I cannot move out of the country but if you send me your account number if will forward half of it to you...." If you have internet you have these scams.

Internet dating has millions of lonely people looking for love and sex - golden opportunities for the psychopath's promiscuity desires and the chance to get money.

Degrees in business, education, etc., are also easily available on the internet. Some degrees are weak in that you get credit for "life experiences" and if you lie and exaggerate enough you can get any degree, even the Ph.D. in a few hours. This situation could reveal a psychopath on each end of the degree program in the student and degree issuer. The psychopath in applying for the easy degree feels he deserves it anyway.

Unfortunately, the legitimacy of such degrees are not thoroughly checked in job applications and the psychopath often gets a job. Sometimes these degrees are forged along with forged experiences and backgrounds, and are often used successfully. Management and group leaders must delve deeply into the background of applicants.

Religious groups, political groups and social groups are excellent targets for the psychopath. Joining or working into the group is easy for the psychopath as the members feel the new person is one of us, believes like us and shares our interest, so he must be all right.

Religious people easily fall into this trap as they feel this person has faith in God so he has to be a good person. Well, the religious group members may feel he has a faith in God but his faith is in his god, a dangerous faith.

When the psychopath is exposed, it is amazing how so many of the people will still not doubt the scammer. Take a look at the many television evangelists who have been exposed and yet the people still cling to them and support them, and refuse to believe the exposure.

Trust is a double edge sword. The cons get their target or targets to trust them. Once the trust is established then the con can manipulate the target. Marriage is a union of trust. They trust each other because it is just the way of marriage. However, it is this trust that makes it so easy to cheat in marriage. Infidelity is based on trust.

Relationships can have the same effect as marriage. The courting of a rich widow leads the psychopath into defrauding the other out of car, money and house. Trust is good, but keep an eye open.

Exposure in organizations is not common as many psychopaths are still plying their trade. They are good at deception so they just roll along. Why mess-up a good thing with good pay, benefits, and power?

If one follows the news one can readily see how some psychopathic CEO's were exposed and left with severance packages, often in the millions. Some were exposed but the company or organization covered it up so that bad publicity would not reign on them. Some were even given letters of good recommendations just to get rid of them. This tactic just gives the psychopath a clear road to another scam.

As we learn more about the corporate psychopath, businesses and other organizations are taking a closer look at their personnel for personality and tactic traits. Thorough checks on resumes for fraudulent claims, conflicting statements, just too smooth in talking, over use of big impressive words, an attitude of trying to cover or hide something can be clues, but only clues, as some clues may just be misleading. Be careful of flattery, misdirection, and failure to answer the question with misdirection or cover-up talk to lead away from the full or correct answer.

Can the work force rehabilitate the psychopath? Not likely. Before exposing the psychopath, management must be 100% sure of facts or disaster and law suits will prevail. When the psychopath is confronted, going "postal" may occur or the psychopath simply admits his behavior and scams and vows to change. Dr. Robert Hare claims that there is little chance of being rehabilitated which the psychopath believes also. Psychopaths may try rehab to play the game, but they have no intention of changing. Their personality traits seem to be well ingrained.

Psychopaths do not change. As they age they often become less active. Punishment does not work. Therapy has not come up with a good treatment program. Psychopaths do not like therapy but will partake to create the image of wanting to be cured and then claiming that they are cured. In fact, some claim that the therapy sessions are helpful in their deceptive act in portraying themselves as normal. They learn what the psychologists or administrators are after so they are able to learn how to act normal. The therapist and psychologist are playing a game to see who wins.

M.E. Thomas in her book, CONFESSIONS OF A SOCIOPATH claims that therapy was a "treasure trove" in teaching her what is expected of her as a normal person. Knowing these expectations made her better at disguising herself and dealing with her manipulation in better and more effective ways.

Big business, corporations, large banks, non-democratic governments, and other competitive enterprises often have a high number of psychopaths running amuck. Babiak and Hare in their book SNAKES IN SUITS: WHEN PSYCHOPATHS GO TO WORK have data that corporations have four times the number of psychopaths than expected by chance.

Organizations and groups often offer goal requirements for the psychopath in authority, power, and money. These factors attract the psychopath.

A good book on the sociopath is CONFESSIONS OF A SOCIOPATH by M.E. Thomas. She calls herself a sociopath because the label psychopath seems too dangerous. She does admit that she is what the psychologists now label as antisocial behavior. She talks and explains many of the traits that are listed and explained preceding this chapter. What is interesting is how she feels that some of the traits are maybe helpful in some ways. Her lack of empathy does not eliminate a concern for some and their feelings but not for her. When she was a trial lawyer a lack of empathy for the opposition was good. Even though she may lack empathy she still helped others like her students as she is now a university professor.

Her other traits that labeled her a sociopath had some good and bad points and as she states she has no regrets on being a sociopath. When young she had a tomboy complex of excitement, fights, roughhousing, stealing, etc. but as she aged these traits also lessened. The following quote give a little insight into her personality.

I am a sociopath. Through dual quirks of genetics and environment, I suffer from what psychologists now refer to as antisocial personality disorder, characterized in the DIAGNOSTIC AND STATISTICAL MANUAL OF MENTAL DISORDERS (DSM) as "a pervasive pattern of disregard for the violation of the rights of others." Key among the characteristics of the diagnosis are a lack of remorse, a penchant for deceit, and a failure to conform to social norms. I prefer to define my sociopathy as a set of traits that inform my personality but don't define me: I am generally free of entangling and irrational emotions, I am strategic and canny, I am intelligent and confident and charming, but I also struggle to react appropriately to other people's confusing and emotion-driven social cues. . . I may have a disorder, but I am not crazy."

She admits to the following that some may think she is crazy. She loves to bike in the city because it can be dangerous. If a car creeps up on her she swipes it with her portable tire pump. If a car cuts her off, she will chase it until she catches it and then swoops in front of the car and stop, forcing the driver to slam on the brakes. Dangerous, yes but it scares hell out of the driver which is her purpose.

When people ask her if they should get tested because they feel they may be sociopathic, she tells them no because once you get the label you can never get rid of it.

In just two years out of law school, her base salary was $170,000 with a double bonus of $90,000 with significant raises every year. Like she says, she is not crazy.

Kevin Dutton in his book "THE WISDOM OF PSYCHOPATHS: WHAT SAINTS, SPIES, SERIAL KILLERS, CAN TEACH US claims it is a thin line between killers like Hannibal Lecter and brilliant surgeons who lack empathy. Sociopaths are primed for success because they are fearless, confident, charismatic, ruthless and focused - qualities that define them as sociopaths but are also "tailor made" for success.

When we think about it, Joan of Arc must of had these traits in order to lead men into war when it was a male dominated society.

This may lead us to the question: "Is the sociopath's brain wired better than the non-sociopath?" So far there is no research to verify this. Maybe Kevin Dutton's claim as to the wisdom of psychopaths has some merit. Look back on history and many great people may well have been psychopaths.

Joel Bakan agrees with Dutton. In his book THE CORPORATION: THE PATHOLOGICAL PURSUIT OF PROFIT AND POWER he says that corporations have the signs of sociopathy. They are amoral, their own interests come first and they even skirt the law for loopholes for company gain. Leading organizations and companies use these traits to their success as some sociopaths have shown leadership, creativity, and communication skills. If the company has lower management personnel and staff who also have the sociopathic traits then the company may get along well. However, sociopaths are kind of individualistic and often not of team mentality.

So, why is business conducive to sociopath leadership? Business is profit based, make the money, and get the power. Profit overrides all. These factors are a magnet to the sociopath.

It is estimated that 10% of Wall Street employees are psychopaths. Some think higher and some lower but the nature of Wall Street has the environment of risk-taking, power, and money. These are attractive to the psychopath.

How about the fall of Enron? No testing was done to determine the psychopathic tendencies of the leaders but indications seem to show a trend or full attention to psychopathy and/or sociopathy.

M. E. Thomas in CONFESSIONS OF A SOCIOPATH claims that the sociopath's brain learns in a chaotic way that is similar to brains with attention deficit disorder. Their brains break up information into small fragments and store it randomly on both sides or hemispheres of the brain. It is believed that this storage factor is the reason that the corpus callosum of the sociopath is longer and skinnier than average because of the high rate of information transmitted between the two hemispheres of the brain.

While we are on the brain, King's College London's Institute of Psychiatry has shown that the brains of sociopathic criminals show less gray matter in the areas of the brain that reveal an understanding of the emotions of others. This means that sociopathic brains show no emotions to words or pictures of violence, rape, disease, etc. The prefrontal cortex of the brain helps to regulate emotions and threats. The amygdala which processes these emotions has fewer connections and this causes impairment of information processing.

Dr. Hervey Cleckley in his book THE MASK OF SANITY says that psychopaths are antisocial yet seem to excel in feelings, desires, hope and love like everyone else. They are indistinguishable or invisible among society. They are cool under pressure, eloquent and unflappable. They have these seemingly positive character traits, but behind the mask of sanity they are manipulators, liars, lack responsibility, are narcissistic, lack emotional bonds, and are promiscuous.

M.E. Thomas claims all these factors are sometimes negative and sometimes positive depending on the situation.

Cleckley devised 16 behavioral factors of a psychopath. Dr. Robert Hare used these traits as a basis for his PSYCHOPATH CHECKLIST.

As we know many psychopaths are not killers, but perhaps they shouldbe called destroyers of people and society.

Let's look at a tycoon businessman. Business seems like the ideal lifestyle for the psychopath and the following people may well be business psychopaths. Much of the literature on these people brings out their successes and accomplishments but little is mentioned as to the emotional side of their actions. So with little to go on we may be able to assume some psychological aspects of the following people.

BERNARD MADOFF

http://en.wikipedia.org/wiki/Bernard_Madoff

Madoff was a former stockbroker, investment advisor, financier and even a non-executive chairman of the NASDAQ stock market. He is now a white collar criminal. His crime is the largest financial fraud in U.S. history under the old Ponzi scheme.

His firm was the Bernard L. Madoff Investment Securities. His main employees were his family members, his brother Peter and Peter's daughter Shana and his two sons, Mark and Andrew.

One day before his arrest in 2008, Madoff confessed to his sons that his firm was a massive Ponzi scheme that defrauded thousands of investors of billions of dollars. He must have been very good at secrecy of his fraud as the family did not know it even though they were highly involved in the operations.

Madoff was busy and very influential in the stock market business. He helped develop NASDAQ and at one time was the largest market maker at NASDAQ. He was active in the NATIONAL ASSOCIATION OF

SECURITIES DEALERS (NASD) where he was Chairman of the Board of Directors and served as a member of the Board of Governors. His background is such that he must have had good access to the knowledge of the stock market and securities. This knowledge must have been helpful to being able to con or sway so many people into fraudulent investments in his company.

Madoff claimed that he should have been caught in 2003 but the investigators were bumblers and never asked the right questions to get the correct and desired answers. The investigators never checked with the Depository Trust Company, a central securities depository for inconsistencies which would easily show a Ponzi scheme. There were six botched investigations in looking for a conviction and some investigators even doubted that he was even trading.

Madoff was very active in politics and giving financial support to candidates. For a man who was only concerned about making money it seems strange to be giving money away unless for political gain or to create the image of being helpful to people.

Although his firm grew into a multi-billion-dollar operation many of the major firms and Wall Street firms would not trade with him as they did not believe his numbers and felt he was not legitimate.

Sheryl Weinstein, a former chief financial officer for Hadassah wrote a book on her investment losses to Madoff in an effort to regain some royalty money to help counter her losses. In the book she confessed to an affair with Madoff.

If we look at Madoff's personality we see some psychopathic tendencies. Like a psychopath his lifestyle was secretive even to his family up until a day before his arrest. Other psychopathic tendencies are:

> 1.
> He involved the family in jobs with the company. He looked after the family. Gangsters in the Mob also did the same and were especially helpful to their offspring, wife and/or mistresses. Perhaps it is a presentation to others that he was really a family man.
>
> He knew the business and was involved with the right people for connections.
>
> He was glib and a master of words in being able to convince people into investing in his fraudulent scheme (PCL-R 1, 2, 4, 5, 7 8).

He was active in politics with his many donations. Ted Bundy and John Wayne Gacy along with other psychopaths were involved in politics in trying to be where the action is (PCL-R 2, 3).

Evidently he had no remorse, empathy or feeling of guilt for his clients. A strong psychopathic tendency (PCL-R 6).

One affair was known of but others may be unknown, so the possibility of promiscuity may be present (PCL-R 11).

Madoff must have had a grandiose sense of self-worth (PCL-R 2).

After his arrest he did apologize, but was he really sincere? Was the apology for his regret or for to show the law he is so sorry that maybe they will lessen his sentence? Perhaps his apology is for getting caught, after all why did he not apologize when he was scamming the money - no feeling of guilt or regret then?

WINSTON CHURCHILL

Churchill was a great orator and naturally had many quotes. Most of his quotes came through the WWII years and as a rallying for the people.

I would say to the House, as I said to those who have joined this Government: 'I have nothing to offer but blood, toil, tears, and sweat."

Here is the answer, which I will give to President Roosevelt... We shall not fail or falter; we shall not weaken or tire. Neither the sudden shock of battle nor the long-drawn trials of vigilance and exertion will wear us down. Give us the tools and we will finish the job.

A pessimist sees the difficulty in every opportunity; an optimist sees the opportunity in every difficulty.

Courage is what it takes to stand up and speak; courage is also what it takes to sit down and listen.

All the great things are simple, and many can be expressed in a single word: freedom, justice, honor, duty, mercy, hope.

We shall defend our island, whatever the cost may be, we shall fight on the beaches, we shall fight on the landing grounds, we shall fight in the fields and in the streets, we shall fight in the hills; we shall never surrender.

We make a living by what we get, but we make a life by what we give. A joke is a very serious thing.

Dictators ride to and fro on tigers from which they dare not dismount. And the tigers are getting hungry.

I have never accepted what many people have kindly said, namely that I have inspired the nation. It was the nation and the race dwelling all around the globe that had the lion heart. I had the luck to be called upon to give the roar.

Never in the field of human conflict was so much owed by so many to so few.


We shall not flag or fail. We shall fight in France, we shall fight on the seas and oceans, we shall fight with growing confidence and growing strength in the air, we shall defend our island, whatever the cost may be, we shall fight on the beaches, we shall fight on the landing grounds, we shall fight in the fields and in the streets, we shall fight in the hills; we shall never surrender.

Churchill's quotes are with the people and not himself in his use of the word, "We" and not "I". Churchill also seems not violent but protective of his people. Some think Churchill was psychopathic with his grandiose self-worth and his glib and manipulative manner, but he had great empathy for his people and the protection of England.

## JACK WELCH

Welch was best known for his successful turnaround of the General Electric Company. He brought the company from 13 billion to several hundred billion. His style and management skills became legendary as he was hard, difficult and even ruthless at times. He was successful and as is so often the case, success overrides methods. He freely fired his managers for not following protocol or the changes he demanded.

His takeover resulted in more than 100,000 employees losing their jobs. Despite this loss of manpower, his streamlining of General Electric prospered with new business operations.

Welch was the epitome of the term, "love him or hate him." Many loved him for success with the company. Shareholders naturally loved him. Many hated him for his cut-throat dealings and lack of concern for the firings of so many people. He was a double edge sword.

Because of Welch's many firings and job losses he was be criticized for a lack of compassion for the middle class and working class people.

In time Welch's earning and assets were questioned during his divorce to his second wife. When offered a retention package of 2.5 million on his retirement he had to refuse it because it was said to make him look greedy. Actually he said he had enough money anyway.

Welch was married three times and his third wife was the result of an affair with a journalist.

And the question is – was Welch a psychopath? Hard to say but there are some indications.

He was glib and persuasive. He was forceful in getting his way.

There is no doubt he had a grandiose sense of self-worth.

He was active and a hard worker with a constant need for stimulation.

He probably was manipulative in getting his own way.

Evidently there seems to be no remorse or guilt on his firings as he believed it was necessary to achieve his goal of money, success and fame.

He was accused of a lack of empathy on the firing of people.

He saw to it that he especially was well compensated for his work in money and benefits. He may well have had a feeling of deserving it.

Some say he had poor behavioral controls with his anger and temper tantrums.

He had three marriages and his third marriage resulted from an affair. Who knows if he had other affairs? This is a common trait with psychopaths.

The above traits may well focus on a psychopath. But, was he a psychopath or just a business man with a goal of making General Electric the best company it could be. If being ruthless was necessary then the end overlooks the means or way.

# CHAPTER FIVE

## LOVE, SEX, LUST AND RELATIONSHIPS

Psychopaths and sociopaths are usually promiscuous, but before we delve into this - what is promiscuous?

Is promiscuous:
Sex with one person many times?
Sex with many persons one time?
Sex with either gender?
Sex with anything or an implement?
Sex with pain, whips, chains, handcuffs, etc.?
Sex with lots of masturbation?
Sex with animals?
Sex with any age?
Sex is a game and the object of all games is to win?
Sex with no discretion of fat, skinny, ugly, diseased, etc.?
Sex through force or rape?
Sex with women only, men only or animals like sheep?

When someone is accused of being promiscuous is it jealousy or the old term of someone who gets more than you?

The term promiscuous is used very loosely. Maybe being promiscuous is simply having more fun than someone else. Maybe it is just a healthy appetite and an unnecessarily label. If promiscuity is in the psychopath's traits it must be evaluated along with the other traits of power, manipulation, and cohersion, to gain information and perhaps even blackmail.

Sex, love and lust are wanted by most people. Many are starved for it and will do almost anything to achieve it. People will buy into almost any line looking for love. Psychopaths know this and use it for their gain. How common is the hustler who eventually gets money, items, automobiles, etc. given to him by his lover only to move on when his goal is achieved. What about the woman who gets a free apartment, jewelry, expensive goods from a man, sometime a married man, so she can live in luxury? Sometimes all this can be achieved by the words, "I love you." These three words can be a double edged sword. They can mean what they say or they can be the forerunner or omen of a con.

Let's take a look at the "sweetheart swindler" who moves from widow to widow milking them of money, cars, motor homes, and many other expensive things. Senior citizens' dances and social clubs give him access to the women, usually the older women who are divorced or widowed. The psychopath has a record of fraud, forgery and theft, in conning many women. He considers himself a humanitarian while admitting to taking their money as he says they got their money's worth out of me. I fulfilled their needs. They got attention, affection, companionship and love. Sometimes we did not even get out of bed. The psychopath sees things differently. The ironic picture is that he did give the women these services!

Psychopaths are deceitful and liars. It is their trait. They use it often because it is so easy. People in love often believe everything. Friends and outsiders can see a relationship not working but the lover can't. Sometimes it takes many physical beatings before the lover realizes what others see.

Psychopaths often have short stormy relationships because the partner realizes things are not working. Some suffer for a long time because of kids and family. Some actually think it is their fault. "I must try harder and it will work out." Some have actually tried hard to please the abusive partner and sadly it sometimes eventually leads to their death.

Some relationship only last a night as they were picked up in a bar or some other location, were charmed and coddled and as the night wore on they were tortured, mutilated, killed, with some even eating their body parts.

Love, sex, and lust can be a killer.

Psychopaths are well versed in the law of infidelity, "A compliment by a stranger has more power than a compliment by a significant other." Significant others are supposed to compliment. A husband compliments his wife as it is expected, but a stranger or friend does not have to compliment. When needed, especially in seduction, the compliments fly, sometimes overdone but it often still works. Compliments do not have to be in words as action will do the job. Opening or holding the door for someone shows manners and respect which women love. A gentle touch to the body can also convey a message and the psychopath knows them all and uses them all.

Quite often the psychopath with his lack of empathy and emotions does not care for the expression of love like a motherly kiss, or a grandparent's hug. They lack the feeling for such but will go along if there is something to be gained. Remember the con man psychopath who goes through all the emotions of love in order to fleece someone of their money or assets. They play the game, but love is not the goal. The goal is money or assets. When the money or assets are achieved the game is over. There is no pain or guilt. The game is won and it is on to the next game. The victim is embarrassed, hurt, and depressed which can lead to serious problems. If the game was scored on a negative to positive continuum or scale the victim would be at the extreme negative and the psychopath would be on the extreme positive.

Love and sex are indirectly related to the psychopath's addiction to power, control, narcissism, and being adored by others, and yet the traits of deception and deceit are vital to the psychopath. It is part of promiscuity and a strong part of seduction. Good seduction artists know how to listen so they can apply the proper compliments and understandings that mean so much to the targeted person.

Promiscuity is the striving for pleasure. Most of the psychopath's traits give pleasure to themselves. It makes them happy with themselves. Sometimes they are happy when they kill someone, a power trip.

Clerkely claims that the psychopath's sex life is impersonal, trivial and poorly integrated. To a certain extent this is true, but sex is so complicated and so much depends on the situation and emotions at the time. We all know this as sex can be turned on or off so quickly.

With some psychopaths, rape is common, and since rape is considered a crime of power and control one can see how this fits into the pattern of the psychopath. Sometimes sex gets into the bizarre world of bondage and pain.

Sex in cults and other similar groups have a strong basis in the ways of the group. Very often sex is unrestricted and unlimited with no denial to anyone. Very often this is in line with the leader who wants this for his own benefit. Some cults may have restrictions but they are often ignored especially by the leader. Some of the leaders are involved with young and very young, children. The wives of others can be free game.

The seduction game in some cults is based on a spiritual or religious influence. It is God's will. This is what God wants. We must not forget that some cults have female leaders and their sexual desires are like the male leaders.

A video of a sexual psychopath claims that the easiest way to get the sex he wanted was to help the victim and when helping the person a trust would develop. He soon got what he wanted.

The history of sex and the sociopath is changing. At one time homosexuality was thought to be connected to sociopathy and other sexual disorders. The original edition of the DIAGNOSTIC AND STATISTICAL MANUAL OF MENTAL DISORDERS (DSM) listed homosexuality as a sociopathic personality disorder. The next edition of DSM sociopathy and homosexuality were no longer linked together. Now in the third edition homosexuality was removed as a mental disorder.

Bisexuality is not a problem with many psychopaths. They just want sex - man, women, animal, object. etc. They have no preference or label; they are an equal opportunity predator. Why would they worry? They have no guilt and only want to pleasure themselves.

Erotic asphyxiation is a sexual high that sociopaths like to receive and give. As orgasm approaches the person is chocked into oxygen deprivation to give a "high". It creates a lightheadedness, erotic sensation throughout the body, an euphoria. It is a dangerous move if carried too far and can result in death but danger is the psychopath's desire.

Robert Hare gives an example of the cunning and deception of the psychopath. An inmate of his had three different files, one said he was psychotic, one said he was normal and the other said he was mildly disturbed. During his interview the inmate said that the psychologists and psychiatrists were air heads. To receive a desired transfer to the psychiatric unit, he faked mental illness on the MMPI hoping for easier time. He didn't like it so he came out normal on his next MMPI and was sent back to the main prison. Later he faked the MMPI for mild disturbances through anxiety and depression. He was given valium pills which he sold to the inmates.

# CHAPTER SIX

# THE SERIAL BULLY

From the Bully Online, web site of the UK National Workplace Bullying Advice line. (www.bullyonline.org/work bully/serial.htm).

This website from the United Kingdom (UK) gives another perspective of the non-killing psychopath. Bullying seems to be a growing trend not just in the UK but most societies. The work place seems to be a common ground in the adult world but children also seem to be learning and using the skills. The question is are the skills learned from adults or is there some genetic quality in the mind which leads people to bullying.

People who bully often exhibit features of a psychopathic personality. Like the psychopath, they have an aversion to rules, regulations, procedures and laws. It is ironic that they cannot conform to these rules but insist others follow the rules perfectly. This seems to prevail with many bosses and managers with the philosophy - do as I say not as I do.

The bully is impulsive and often reckless. They cannot accept minor frustrations or mistakes with their associates. These characteristics often lead to unstable relationships and a private life of uncertainty.

Experiences often do not provide opportunity to learn for the future in interpersonal skills, social, communication and behavioral skills. What the psychopath does learn is how to cover his deception, lies, etc. in maintaining his accountability.

If we go through an adjective checklist, we find the following adjectives or short phrases that pertain to the psychopath:

Liar, Jekyll and Hyde personality, deception, charm, glib, good verbal skills, smooth, slimy, lack of reliability, lack of trust, emotionally immature, inappropriate attitudes to sexual matters, sexual behavior and bodily functions (anal attitude), intimacy problems, arrogant, deep prejudices, arrogance, self-opinionated, superior sense of entitlement, being untouchable, control freak, love to be critical of others, rambles and changes topics or trend of thoughts in conversations, evasive, escaped accountability, creates conflict, vindictive, belittle and undermine people, loves to deny people's rights, manipulative, know-it all's, can be petty, mean, financially untrustworthy, a taker and not a giver, convinced of the superiority, confuse bullying with leadership, project a false reality of themselves, like the psychopath they know the words but not the song.

That is quite an array of traits. Some may not have all of them but one can readily see the picture. We must be careful in over-reacting to the traits. TRAITS are characteristics that are in the personality all the time and are chronic. STATES are characteristics that prevail for the situation. One may show anger, rage, and arrogance in a certain situation or problem, but only in that situation. That may well be normal and not a chronic characteristic to all problems. Do not let an infrequent rage label the person as in some circumstances the rage may be well deserved.

The web site (listed above) gives detailed analyses of four types of serial bullies, the attention-seeker, the wannabe, the Guru and the Sociopath. The following is a very short summary.

## The Attention-Seeker
Their motivation and goal is to be the center of attention. When in groups, they like to dominate the conversation or situation. Their mind set is one of manipulation, narcissism and being a control freak. These tie in with striving for being the center of attention. They are the world and all rotates around them. Revenge and malice are high in their traits.

## The Wannabe

Their motivation is their name. They want to be the authority, the professional and the leader. They wannabe, but in reality they lack the knowledge and ability. They try to project the image but just can't pull it off for the long term. Eventually it catches up. Deception is their key and is easily seen in trying to cover their incompetence.

## The Guru
The Guru is very task focused but has a mindset of confusion, and a lack of understanding in how others think and feel. Again, the lack of empathy keeps coming up. Usually their malice is low in respect to them maintaining an image, a false image; this can change when they have high narcissistic or psychopathic tendencies.

## The Socialized Psychopath or Sociopath
Aliases include the corporate psychopath, workplace psychopath, industrial psychopath and administrative psychopath. They continually search for power and personal gain even if it means embezzlement. They have strong malice and revenge tendencies.

Serial bullies also have other labels as many traits are found in other disorders. Labeling a person is difficult because of the common traits with each disorder. Even psychologists and psychiatrists often give different labels of disorders to the same person.

The similar traits are:
Antisocial Personality Disorder (APD)
This was often the label before the term psychopathy developed. There is a pattern of disregard for rights of others.

Failure to conform to social norms and laws.

Constant lying, deceitful and conning others for personal gain.

Impulsive, with a lack of planning.

Aggressive with physical fights and assaults.

Disregard for safety of others.

Disregard for financial obligations.

Irresponsibility.

Lack of loyalty.
Often bullying is learned in school.

Narcissistic Personality Disorder (NPD)
The serial bully shows traits of Narcissistic Personality Disorder.

A pattern of grandiosity, need for admiration and lack of empathy.

Strong belief in self-importance.

Fantasies of success, power, brilliance, beauty and love.

A belief in being special.

Requires excessive admiration from others as well as from himself.

A belief in entitlement, as being special and deserving.

His entitlement gives him the right to exploit others.

Lack of empathy.

Arrogant is willing to show it.

Paranoid Personality Disorder (PPD)
Paranoia is common with the serial bully. There is a distrust and suspicion of others.

Believes others are exploiting him or her even with lack of proof.

Doubts loyalty of others.

A fear in trusting others. Fails to reveal too much of themselves so that others may not use such knowledge against them at a future time.

Bears grudges.

Perceives attacks in comments made in humor or with no intent. They respond with anger and hostility.

Very suspicious of spouse or ex-lover even with no proof.

Borderline Personality Disorder (BPD)
Often believed to be a result of a childhood abuse, intentional or unintentional.

Frantic efforts to avoid real or imagined abandonment.

A pattern of unstable and intense interpersonal relationships.

Problems with self-image and a sense of self.

Impulsivity with spending, sex, substance abuse, reckless driving and binge eating.

Some trends to suicide behavior, threats and self-mutilating behavior.

Moody.

Feelings of emptiness.

Difficulty in controlling anger, temper tantrums, physical fighting.

Sever dissociative symptoms.

As we review the traits of the bully, we notice many traits coincide with the psychopath and sociopath.

# CHAPTER SEVEN

# EARLY YEARS OF THE PSYCHOPATH

The first thing we must realize is that psychopaths can come from good, stable families as well as from the bad home life with dangerous environmental factors.

Parents can do little to change or alter the growing psychopath's personality. Many parents have used all resources available like family services, psychologists, psychiatrists, counselors and therapists and yet little is gained, if anything. Even though they are children their manipulative skills and lies are very good, and they often fool the psychologists. The parents are confused, wondering if they did something wrong with their kids.

Problems can be noticed at a very young age, like even 5 or 6 years old. From here, it just escalates. Psychopathic children often know what is right and wrong but they do not care, as they have no feeling for others. Punishments, threats, and pleas are of no assistance.

As the child grows older, he or she learns manipulation, intimidation and other antisocial skills and how to refine them to an art. Bullying in school and away from school, like in playgrounds, also is shown at this age.

Dangerous activities will occur unless the child's psychopathy is constantly supervised. A nine-year old boy pushed a toddler into the swimming pool at a motel and then pulled up a chair to watch it drown or just to see what would happen. When asked why, he calmly said, "just curious". This is an extreme example, as not all psychopathic children are killers in the same way not all psychopathic adults are killers.

Labeling children with the psychopath label is a touchy practice, as many cannot accept the fact it occurs in children, but research indicates that it does. Psychopathy does not just spring up in later life. In fact, many parents have verified the research when their offspring diagnosed as a psychopath proven in later life. The parents have lived through the disorder in knowing something was wrong all along. Some parents have even admitted to fears of serious threats to health and life.

Psychopathic children even scored high in the Psychopathic Checklist - Revised. Such children are more difficult, willful, aggressive, deceitful, and have difficulty in relating or getting close to avoid being influenced and taking instructions.

In their early school years they:

Show repetitive lying.

Show indifference to the feelings of others.

Show a defiance of parents, teachers and rules.

Show a trend for trouble.

Unresponsive to punishment or reprimands.

Show petty theft to parents, other children and shoplifting.

Show aggressive tendencies, bullying and physical fighting.

Show truancy, late nights and absences from home.

Show malice to hurting or killing animals.

Show early experimentation with sex.

Show up in vandalism and arson.

Dr. Hare cites an interesting case study. A mother tells Dr. Hare about her 5-year-old daughter who tried to flush her cat down the toilet. The mother caught her but the child showed no concern just a peeve for being caught. After telling the husband, the husband talked to the child and the child denied it happened. The child was always trying to have her own way with either being sweet or having a tantrum. She lied even though she knew the parents knew she was lying. When the girl was seven, the mother had a son and the girl would tease the baby in cruel ways. At 13 she was truant, sexually active and into theft.

So far intervention with children psychopaths is very limited if it works at all. However, if there is any chance of helping, it would have to be started at this age, as this may be the only chance for success.

Parents, teachers, sport coaches are probably the first to recognize these characteristics and should be the first to recommend help. Of course, they have to be trained, not for treatment, but for recognizing the problem and where to send the kid for help. They must be warned and must realize they are not the solution, trained people may be the solution.

Recognition of such traits is not easy, as one must distinguish if the trait is a psychopathic trait or just an exaggerated form of normal behavior. This is not easy. Things like egocentricity, deceit, and manipulation are common to a degree with most kids as they are still immature.

In trying to treat psychopaths, we look to what starts the problem and where does it come from. One of the theories is that it is genetic and biological (nature). The other theory is that it is the result is from social environment (nurture). It is believed that the answer lies somewhere between these two extremes, but where between the extremes?

In answer to the nature (born, in the blood, genetic) versus nurture (the environment) some feel that the traits are genetic at conception but the traits are regulated by the environment.

The Texas Adoption Project found that in a longitudinal study of over 500 adopted children, the individuals resemble their birth mother, who they never see or know, more than they resemble their adoptive parents. This shows some genetic factors. Since the word 'more' is used instead of 'all' it must mean that some environmental factors are involved.

Research into the possibility of brain damage has shown that brain damage, while young, does not lead to psychopathy. Families with several children, within the same environment, can have one of their kids labeled as a psychopath. The bad apple is in constant trouble at school, the law, and life, while the others are model citizens. This happens and seems to negate the theory that social factors and environment cause psychopathy.

Social environment, neglect, drugs, maltreatment, etc., seems to show no convincing evidence of causing psychopathy. These factors do cause problems but not necessarily psychopathy. As previously mentioned the rehabilitation of psychopaths has limited success as 80% of psychopaths that are released from prison are soon back in prison.

The dilemma persists. What is the cause? How can we treat?

Psychologists use the term normal for the non-sociopaths, but do the sociopathic children growing up think they are normal while the others "labeled normal kids" are not normal? A kid is not a psychologist, which may be good, but how does the sociopathic kid understand the fact that other kids do not think and act as he or she does?

Oddly, at present, we do not know how to treat the sociopath or psychopath. And if we did, we have to cope with the fact that the sociopath usually does not want to be treated. You can lead a horse to water but you can't make him drink.

A sociopath, M.E. Thomas in her book CONFESSIONS OF A SOCIOPATH claimed that they would not mind if their children were sociopaths as they would work with them but their concern is not with their child but how society would treat their child.

# CHAPTER EIGHT

# THE DANGEROUS MIND

CULTURAL DIFFERENCES
According to Martha Stout, in her book THE SOCIOPATH NEXT DOOR, Asian cultures show antisocial disorders at an average of 0.03 to 0.04 percent of their population. Western cultures have an average of 4.0 percent. This means that Western cultures have 133 percent more antisocial disorders than Asian cultures. Unfortunately, the reason for these differences is not known.

All cultures have psychopaths, sociopaths and other mental problems, now and throughout their history. Jane M. Murphy, a psychiatric anthropologist, is quoted in THE SOCIOPATH NEXT DOOR telling about the Inuit (Eskimo) in North West Alaska concept of "kunlangeta." The kunlangeta is their concept of a sociopath, as their word means, "the mind knows what to do but does not do it." The kunlangeta lies, cheats, steals, refuses to go hunting, relies on others for everything and when the men go hunting he stays home and sexually preys on the women. The Inuits had a solution. They would insist that he go hunting with them and with no witnesses, he was pushed off the ice into the freezing water. Problem solved.

Members of the Yoruba tribe in Africa called their cold souls, "arankan" meaning a person who goes his own way regardless of others, is uncooperative, full of malice and is bullheaded.

Some cultures have fewer sociopaths than others. Sociopathy is rare in eastern Asia, particularly in Japan and China. Taiwan has a 0.03 to 0.14 percent while the Western world has 4 percent, which is one in twenty-four people. Frightfully, it is increasing in the United States, but it may just be that such mental conditions are more frequently diagnosed in the U.S.A.

Although it may not fit the definition of culture it is interesting to note that M. E. Thomas in her book THE CONFESSIONS OF A SOCIOPATH says that some of the most amoral and manipulative people she has met were in law school with her. They had little regard for others. Everything was to optimize their advantage on everything, even trivial matter like who had a better breakfast. Research has proven that this is accurate along with business and other groups and organizations as such groups have an overabundance of sociopaths.

Law and courtroom drama of prosecutor versus defender is a game, excitement of who wins. Win at all cost for big money. This is the sociopath's goal.


NICCOLE MACHIAVELLI

Machiavelli became a personality trait from his book THE PRINCE written in 1514. In recent years, the book's popularity grew and was adopted by many groups, organizations and especially the business world. In regards to the business world, the book become significant because many leaders showed psychopathic tendencies and the book supported their personality.

According to Thiessen, Machiavellianism "is just short of an illness of the mind - a form of disturbed genius - centering on disturbed narcissism ...diminished sympathy ... sometimes charming and often callous... selfish human behaviors...which became the label for Machiavellian behaviors. The case can be made that Machiavellian traits overlap psychopathic behaviors".

The following is Thiessen's description of the Machiavellian individual. You will notice the many psychopathic traits. Here is what Thiessen says:

Not all my encounters with Machiavellian individuals have been delightful. These people, usually male (three to one), share traits with common street psychopaths, but are unique in degrees or narcissism, intelligence, competitive skills, and passions for winning.

They also have a sense of destiny, are generally low in affect and empathy, and high is sensation seeking, persistence and grandiosity. They seem destined for success, but also lean toward lugubrious faces.

In distinction to street psychopaths, Machiavellians often drive culture to higher levels of expression. They rarely end up in prison, almost never murder, and don't end up in the county morgue. Instead, within this heterogeneous group we find our greatest writers, artists, and intellectuals, scientists and educators, hard driving entrepreneurs, professional experts and solipsistic (the self is the only reality) and politicians.

I consider the Mach as a psychopath with distinction, an enriched version of the common psychopath, but more intelligent, controlled and productive.

Machiavellian traits are narcissistic, charismatic, hedonistic, risk-taker, dishonest, promiscuous, no guilt or remorse, short-term sexual relations, law anxiety, self-destructive, needs excitement, grandiose, drug user, no fear, selfish and low empathy. What more can be said?

Before we look at identifying a psychopath, let's look at some strange labels of social disorders. At a Scientology banquet Lady Margaret McNair, head of the UK branch of the CCHR, Scientology anti-psychiatry wing, made a speech on new mental disorders, which they hoped to be included in the DSM-DSM-V. Scientology is not supportive of the psychiatry industry. For example, her disorder was that if you honked your horn in anger with uncontrollable rage, an extreme expression of anger, disproportionate to the situation then you suffer from Intermittent Explosive Disorder.

Next, we have Internet Disorder that may mean negative repercussions like arguments, lying, poor achievement, social isolation and fatigue. The DSM-V says too much time on the internet may be a symptom of depression.

A fight with your spouse is a Relational Disorder.

If you are lazy, then you suffer from Sluggish Tempo Disorder.

She talked further on Binge Eating Disorder, Passive-aggressive Personality Disorder, and Post-Traumatic Embitterment Disorder.

Are we becoming a "Label Society?"

# CHAPTER NINE

# HOW TO IDENTIFY A PSYCHOPATH

Wolf Thiessen in SLIP-UPS AND THE DANGEROUS MIND gives a short list of psychopathic traits and how to identify a psychopath. Be careful, as these traits are common in many non-psychopaths. Identification is in the degree of severity of the trait and how the traits fit into the overall pattern and cluster of traits.

Lifestyle trait clusters:
Unusual dress, unkempt, tattoos, tacky, can be humorous, sarcastic, ironic, loud, and obnoxious. Too much self-confidence, overuse of the word "I" and too ambitious.

Excitement and interest in extreme sports, drugs, gambling, alcohol, rock and roll, body building, martial arts, fast cars, motorcycles, risky investments, muscular body type, with possible high levels of testosterone and dopamine.

Has aggressive moves, likes guns and weapons, brags about confrontations.

Reduced fear, looks right through you, cool in stress, not easily shocked.

Loves to party, inability to keep a job or maintain long-term residence and relationships, dislikes formal or traditional education.

Too much confidence, blames others for faults, makes fun of others, too prominent in the social websites.

Work difficulties, lies in resume, experience, tend to bully tactics, not appreciative of other's work.

Early abuse of animals, history of conduct disorders.

Narcissist.

No interest in children or long-term relationships, or family matters.

Here is a list of individual traits: pushy, especially with sex, lack of empathy, callous, disregard of others, lateness and disregard for appointments, self-centered, glib, consistent liar, blames others, likes to orate especially about himself, easily bored, manic-depressive, compulsive, charming when needed, wants quick gratification.

A list of social traits: promiscuous, few long term friends, lack of long relationships, petty criminal behavior, superficially gregarious when needed, superiority feelings, cult participation, and condescension, aloof, secretive especially on his or her background.

Martha Stout in her THE SOCIOPATH NEXT DOOR says that in her 25 years of patient stories she often has to answer the question, "who can I not trust." She claims, "The best clue is, of all things, the pity play. The most reliable sign, the most universal behavior of unscrupulous people is an appeal to our sympathy."

She discovered this to her surprise while as a graduate student interviewing a psychopath who was not violent but preferred to con people out of their money through elaborate fraudulent investments. When she asked the psychopath "What is important to you in your life? What do you want more than anything in your life? His reply surprised her, "Oh, that's easy. What I like better than anything else is when people feel sorry for me. The thing I really want more than anything else out of life is people's pity."

As she learned later with more such interviews, the reason for pity is so obvious, too obvious to readily notice. "Good people let pathetic individuals get by with murder, so to speak, and therefore any sociopath wishing to continue with his game, whatever it happens to be, should play repeatedly for none other than pity. Pity from good people is carte blanch. When we pity, we are at least for the moment defenseless... our emotional vulnerability when we pity is used against us by those who have no conscience."

We remember Ted Bundy who would wear a false cast on his arm and get a woman to help him unload his car. The woman was the victim of the "have pity on me," ploy.

Pity and sympathy are acceptable when trouble and misfortune happen to deserving people. They deserve our concern and help. However, pity is not deserved by the manipulative sociopath who use it for personal gain. The battered and abused wife is a constant reminder of how the psychopath/sociopath beats his wife and then goes into his cry for sympathy, his routine of overdone apologies and the act of being so sorry and that it will never happen again. However, it does happen again because the wife feels pity and sorry for the sociopath and often outrageously blames herself for his outburst. Quite often the wife will say that "Maybe I brought it on."

If any of these traits pop-up be wary. Be a little safe. Check out backgrounds from reliable sources. Remember - proof, proof and more proof.

Identifying a Psychopath

Identifying a psychopath is not easy as even the experts have been duped and fooled. Psychopaths are just good at deceiving people. They feel that they are so good and confident at it that they do not need therapy. Therapy just does not seem to work as often the therapist is duped and believes the act of the psychopaths and their lies.

Here is an example in the book THE PSYCHOPATH TEST by Jon Ronson on identifying the sane from the psychopath. A man was arrested for assault and battery. While in jail, he was advised by the other prisoners to claim madness and he would be sent to the county hospital with Sky TV and Play Station. Nurses would even serve pizza.

He decided that the best course of action was to fake madness to get out of a prison sentence of five or more years. He reasoned that this would get him into a comfortable local hospital with easy living. He was sent to Broadmoor, an asylum for hardened and dangerous people in the criminal world.

Now that he is in the asylum, he is trying to convince them he is sane, normal, and not mad and was just trying to get out of the severe sentence. The more he tries to convince psychiatrists he is not mad the more the psychiatrists are convinced that he is mad. The man claims the environment in the asylum is driving him crazy.

Now the guy tries to convince people that he is sane. This is very difficult as it is easier to convince one that you are "crazy". In his effort to appear normal he would talk to people in a normal manner about normal things like football and what's on TV, but it did not seem to work. Unfortunately, he subscribes to NEW SCIENTIST, as he likes the scientific breakthroughs and other interesting research. In conversations with a nurse he tells her about an article where the U.S. Army is training bumblebees to sniff out explosives. Later on reading his medical notes it says "he thinks bees can sniff out explosives." It is not revealed how he got the medical notes but it does show how easily words or ideas can be misinterpreted.

His efforts at acting normal, even offering to help out weeding the asylum garden, This was interpreted as being only able to behave in the environment of the asylum so they keep him there. He should not be released, as he needs the asylum.

A psychiatrist said that his faking madness to get out of a prison sentence is a deceitful and manipulative act you would expect from a psychopath. Faking that the brain is going wrong is a sign that the brain is wrong. When one thinks about this reasoning, wouldn't a normal person try to find a way to get out of prison? Isn't this why the accused plead not guilty and hire lawyers to get an acquittal? The plea "not guilty" is faking it even if they are guilty or not. It is a faking of guilt.

Many killers have tried faking mental illness and have succeeded in being assigned to a mental hospital where they believed that they can act normal and be released. However, the problem is that when they act normal and behave as being cured, very few believe them. We must remember that proving normalcy is difficult, extremely difficult.

Ian Brady, the Moors Murderer (BBC NEWS MAGAZINE, June 27, 2013), killed five children. He claims he was using method-acting techniques to fool the doctors and psychologists. The staff at Ashworth Hospital says Brady is schizophrenic and must stay and receive care. When you kill five children, it seems when faking or not faking mental illness, you have a serious problem and should not be released.

In 2007, Stuart Harling was jailed for life for the murder of a nurse in Essex. His lawyers tried to convince the jury of his personality disorders, which he exhibited in court with his shouting, throwing paper files and making threats. The jury did not buy it. One has to wonder if the lawyers put him up to the behavior in court to verify his personality disorder.

In 1996, James Lindsay was sentenced to life for murdering a 15-year-old girl. While awaiting trial he wrote a friend that he had a cunning plan to be admitted into Carstairs Mental Hospital and in eight years, he would be released as cured.

Kenneth Bianchi, the Hillside Strangler, killer of a dozen young women in California, amazingly convinced several experts - even under hypnosis - that he had an alter ego called "Steve" and it was Steve who committed the crimes. Evidently, if the experts agreed on a diagnosis of multiple personality, Bianchi would be able to plead not guilty. Martin Orne, an expert on hypnosis uncovered Bianchi's ruse. Orne claimed that multiple personality disorders had at least three personalities so Bianchi developed "Billy" to give him the three personalities.

Bianchi studied his acting traits. His house had many textbooks on psychology, behavioral science, and hypnosis and police procedures law. His favorite movies were Sybil and Three Faces of Eve, with multiple personalities. He studied his trade.

Bianchi's act was good as he fooled several experts, but not the police. It is interesting to note that on his sentencing the judge said that Bianchi was aided and abetted by the psychiatrists who believed his act.

Several studies in the U.S.A. have shown that about 7% of psychiatric disorders are being faked and the percentage is even higher in criminal cases and could go as high as 22%.

Determining the faking of mental illness is difficult, but a few keys have proven helpful. Overstating and exaggeration of their symptoms creates an unrealistic picture. Fakers like to talk about their hallucinations so the psychiatrists look for inconsistencies and exaggerations. Some psychiatrists are able to lead the accused into making claims that are not possible to indicate lying.

Let us have another look at psychiatry's wisdom. In 1851, an American physician Samuel Cartwright identified a disorder "drapetomania" that occurred in slaves only. Drapetomania's symptom was the desire to run away. The cure was to whip the devil out of them, as the whipping would prevent running away in the future.

Jon Ronson tells of a CCHR video, PSYCHIATRY: AN INDUSTRY OF DEATH in which the DVD said, "In every city, every state, every country, you will find psychiatrists committing rape, sexual abuse, murder and fraud."

This video is extremely controversial. It is put out by the Church of Scientology which itself is controversial.

When we think about it how would you prove that you are sane? This is a true story. A professor at an Iowa University has 31 psychiatric students in training. He arranges with an asylum to admit the students as patients so that they can feel what it is like to be assigned to living in an asylum. The head of the asylum was the only person outside of the professor who knew of the arrangement. When the time came for the students to be released to go back to school, only one student was fit for release. The other students could not show proof of sanity. What the psychologists could not determine, the asylum inmates could. The inmates knew something was up as they were able to identify the students as being normal. Maybe we need role reversal by letting the abnormal patients determine the new patients on entering the asylum.

Along similar lines David Rosenhan in his book ON BEING SANE IN INSANE PLACES did an experiment with seven normal friends. He wanted to demonstrate how useless psychiatrists were. He gave his seven friends who never had any psychiatric problems a pseudonyms and fake occupation. They traveled across America to different mental hospitals. Each told the attending on duty psychiatrist that they were hearing a voice in their head that said the words, "empty," "hollow," and "thud." That was the only lie they could tell and they would otherwise act normally. All eight, Rosenhan included, were immediately diagnosed as insane and admitted into the hospital. Seven were diagnosed as schizophrenic and one was manic-depressive. It took two months for them to be released and only by admitting they were insane and then pretended they were better.

The ending to the experiment is what is interesting. Rosenhan was accused of faking insanity and using trickery to deceive the psychiatrists. One of the hospitals told Rosenhan to send some more fakes and they would be able to spot them easily. Rosenhan agreed. A month later the hospital in a proud declaration announced they had discovered 41 fakes. A happy Rosenhan then revealed that he had sent no one to the hospital. I guess 41 mental illnesses beat the system and are wandering around society quite happy.

But lies can often trip up the psychopath, and this is why one must look for conflicts in the message. In the book THE SOCIOPATH NEXT DOOR, by Martha Stout, she gives a common example of such a conflict.

A secretary sued a company she worked for when her boss, forcing her to sit on his lap, broke her arm. The boss's statement was, "She's insane. She broke her own arm. She struggled with me, the stupid bitch. Why the hell did she put up a fight?" He lies that he did not break the arm. He cannot understand her objection to his request. Psychopaths want their own way. It was her fault she fought me. Psychopaths and sociopaths want to control others. They have to win the situation.

Psychopaths and sociopaths can beat the lie detector test because the lie detector cannot measure lies. The lie detector measures emotions and emotions may, and we mean may, reveal a lie. Psychopaths and sociopaths have no empathy or emotions for other people so that means the lie detector cannot measure emotions because there are no emotions. Besides, the lie detector is not admissible in court as the reliability is 60 to 70% accurate, only if the administer is exceptionally good.

Marshall McLuhan said that the medium is the message and how the message is delivered is often more important than the message. This means look carefully at the medium.

In the book, A FIRST RATE MADNESS, by S. Nassir Ghaemi a Professor of Psychiatry at Tufts

University, claims that the best leaders in troubled times are often touched by madness. With periodic depression and thoughts of suicide, Winston Churchill, Mahatma Gandhi and Abraham Lincoln are all examples of outstanding leadership. By being insensitive to suffering, they are able to lead to the needs of the moment. Some think this is a little exaggeration but when we look at the traits of the psychopath and Machiavellian people there seems to be a possible correlation.

Identifying the sociopath or psychopath can often result in the circle effect of going around and around. For example:

Why did this person do these terrible things?

It is because he is a psychopath.

How do you know he is a psychopath?

Because he did these terrible things.

Once again, the brilliance of the psychologist shines through.

The American Psychiatric Association who author the DSM do not use the terms psychopathy or sociopathy. It seems they prefer the term Antisocial Personality

Disorder (ASPD). The World Health Organization's INTERNATIONAL STATISTICAL CLASSIFICATION OF DISEASES AND RELATED HEALTH PROBLEMS also omits the word sociopathy but uses Dissocial Personality Disorder. Yet we wonder how the terms psychopathy and sociopathy are not in either book yet the psychologists and psychiatrists keep using the terms freely? Does this make psychopathy and sociopathy a phantom diagnosis?

# CHAPTER TEN

# DEALING WITH THE SOCIOPATH

Now that we have identified the sociopath, how do we deal with them? Martha Stout in THE SOCIOPATH NEXT DOOR gives some procedures.

Accept the fact that some are sociopaths and they do not have a special or sinister look. They often look normal.

Sociopaths lie so be careful of the image they present.

If a problem occurs three times it may be dangerous. For example, one lie may not be serious, two lies may mean something but three lies show a consistent pattern. Watch out.

Question authority. People are often afraid to question authority. Do it.

Be careful of flattery. Flattery is a signal someone wants something.

If fear is sensed, be careful. Your instincts may be telling you something.

Do not compete with the sociopath or be lured into their web. Get out.

The best solution in coping with the sociopath is avoidance.

Do not let sympathy or pity enter into the picture.

Be careful with second chances. Remember the three times rule. If it happens twice then something is up.

Watch out when they say, "You owe me." you do not owe them anything.

Do psychopathic killers look evil? No. They look normal and some are even very good looking. Hitler looked comical, like Charlie Chaplin, until he became well known for evil. Ten Bundy was handsome and had women with marriage proposals despite his killing instincts. Lizzie Borden was not bad looking either. This means that one must not depend on looks to determine personality.

# PART TWO

## PSYCHOPATHS WHO KILL

# CHAPTER ELEVEN

# SOLDIERS, POLICE, SPIES, GOVERNMENT AGENTS

Not all killers are psychopaths. Some are paid to kill. Soldiers, police, spies, and government agents are in this category. Some may be in this category because they like the possibility for unrestrained killing. The mercenary soldiers are fighting for this thrill and the money. They fight for any country.

Some non-psychopaths, after the killing spree in wars, will suffer from post-traumatic stress disorder (PTSD). The stress gets to them and they have a difficult adjustment after their release from service. This may be where the psychopath has an advantage in that killing, taking life, the pain of others is no concern to him. Such people can walk away with no guilt as they are alive and that is all that matters.

The psychopath who can kill without guilt, anguish or empathy can make an excellent soldier. Mercenary soldiers may well be along these lines. Do they really do it for the money? The psychopath's traits of adventure, danger, and excitement may well override the money factor.

These warriors, or soldiers, are in all societies, regardless of religion. Religion and its criteria of love thy neighbor, help other people, and promote God's will of love and peace has never stopped a war. In fact, it may have just the opposite effect in that many wars are about religion and killing the people who do not believe as they do.

In battle, psychopaths are fearless and cold-blooded. The take risky chances and often succeed. They are brave and often heroic. Leaders may not like psychopaths in their group but in war and dangerous situations, you may have to like them, as they may well be your road to safety. People who can kill with no guilt are rare but are valuable in war.

Lt. Col. Dave Grossman in his book, ON KILLING, says, "Whether called sociopaths, sheepdogs, warriors, or heroes, they are there, they are a distinct minority, in times of danger a nation needs them desperately."

As we know, psychopathic killers have no emotions or usually show no emotions or empathy, unless they act it. In the book THE PSYCHOPATHIC TEST by Jon Ronson, he relates a story about an interview with a psychopathic killer. The psychopath was shown a picture of a frightened face and was asked to identify the emotion. The psychopath replied that he did not know the emotion but the face was the face just before he killed someone.

Jon Ronson, in PSYCHOPATH TEST tells of visiting Broadmoor asylum and meeting one of the inmates. He had read the inmate's dossier with a history of raping women, killing them and biting their nipples off. The dossier was "hideous reading." The psychiatrist told him that the inmate would charm him. As said, he was very charmed by the inmate. He was "fanciable, good looking, in peak physical condition, and had a very macho manner. It was raw sex appeal. I could completely understand why the women he had killed went with him."

Ronson also tells of Joseph Fredericks, released from Oak Ridge in 1983, who within a few weeks had used a knife when attacking a teenage girl and sodomized a 10-year-old boy. Back in the asylum and on being released again he attacked an 11-year-old boy and then he abducted and raped another 11-year-old boy. When the police caught him he said, "He was such a nice boy, why did he have to die.

Peter Woodstock (http://en.wikipedia.org/wiki/Peter_Woodcock) was put up for adoption and lived in several foster homes. He was abused while young. In 1956 and 1957, he murdered three young children. He was assigned to

Oak Ridge, a psychiatric facility in Ontario, Canada. His therapy concluded that he was greatly improved so they moved him to a medium-security hospital in Brockville, Ontario. While there, he fell in love with an inmate, Dennis Kerr, but Woodstock stabbed Kerr to death when Kerr refused his sexual advances. During his trial, he said he did it to see what effect a hatchet would have on a body.

Woodstock in defending himself claimed that the treatment program made him more adept in manipulating others. Other psychopaths have projected this claim. It is not their fault. The therapists and psychiatrists unknowingly trained the psychopath in manipulation by exposing what they wanted.

How about this one. A man killed another man over a bar tab. When interviewed his cold response was, "Anybody could have seen I was in a rotten mood that night." Here we go again with the, "It's not my fault" excuse.

Who is worse, the psychopathic killers or the psychopaths in business, religion and politics? One answer seems to be killers ruin families while the others ruin society. Look at the recession years of the early 2000's and on. Banks, businesses, TV evangelists, etc. where exposed for fraudulent working and stealing. Many people lost houses, money, etc.

and some even lost trust in their religion. For many, life became a nightmare.

A teenage girl lured a small child outside to play. She strangled the girl and then slit her throat to watch the blood drain. She then buried the child. On returning home, she wrote in her journal how exciting it was. She then went to church.

James Fallon is a neuroscientist and professor at University of California - Irvine where he studies biological roots of behavior. He is famous for his studies on the brain scans of killers. His mother told him he was Lizzie Borden's cousin, a notorious killer. He checked his family and everyone was normal except for him. On telling this information to his family, the family was not surprised. They knew he was a little different. He did not turn out as a killer as some think it was because of a wonderful family rearing, but not all psychopaths are killers.

# CHAPTER TWELVE

# FAMOUS PSYCHOPATHIC KILLERS

The following is a sample of killers with their PSYCHOPATH CHECK LIST - REVISED (PCL-R) scores. As stated earlier, a score of 30 is strong indication of psychopathic tendencies. In the following examples, the scores could be higher but some possible situations are not mentioned so no score is available, but looking at the short summary of the people, we can still see a high score.


**TED BUNDY**: total PCL-R score 30
Murderer, serial killer, rapist.
Born: 1946, Burlington, Vermont
Executed 1989. Florida State Prison, Starke, Florida

Bundy was born out of wedlock. This was a scandal to his mother's parents, which was a common reaction at this time in history. Bundy was delivered at a home for unwed mothers in Vermont. They soon moved to Philadelphia to hide the past. He was raised as the adopted son of the grandparents. He was led to believe his mother was his sister.

Later, Ted and the mother Eleanor, moved to Tacoma, Washington. Here she married Johnnie Bundy and had several more children. It appears that family life was fairly normal.

Bundy was a shy child but bright and intelligent. He got along well with his teachers, but not so well with his fellow students. As he aged, he was fascinated with knives. He liked peeking into other people's windows, a "Peeping Tom" with the hope of seeing sexual acts and other happenings that may be of interest. This peeping may well be the beginning of a promiscuous lifestyle and interest in sex (PCL-R #11), characteristics of psychopaths. He also indulged in stealing things he wanted (PCL-R #12, #18) and had no guilt or remorse about it (PCL-R #6).

While in college, he fell in love with a pretty, wealthy, young woman but was devastated after the breakup. She had all the attributes, money, class, influence, power, that he wanted or any psychopath wanted (PCL-R #9). Later, it was noted that many of his victims had a resemblance to his college girlfriend. Some think he may be acting out revenge, as he was physically brutal with the rape of his victims.

With the start of his killing rampage, he became more confident and arrogant (PCL-R #2, #3, #6, #20). He became active in social circles and politics, which is a good source for meeting women (PCL-R #3, #11). His charm got him a letter of recommendation to law school in Utah from the Governor of Washington for his work on the political campaign (PCL-R #1).

Around this time, it was noticed that several women in the Seattle and nearby Oregon were missing and there was no reason or clues to follow. Reports stated that some of the victims were last seen with a young, dark haired man with a name, something like Ted. This description certainly did not narrow the field of investigation.

Bundy showed creativity in luring his victims with guile, charm, flattery and pity (PCL-R #1, #2, #4, #5, #8)  He would often fake injury and even use fake casts on his arms or legs to gain the victim's pity to help him in carrying groceries to his apartment, etc. (PCL- R #1, #4, #5). It must be remembered that with all his dealings he shows no empathy of concern with the future victim (PCL-R #6, #8).

While attending law school in Utah it was again noticed that many women were missing, just like in the Seattle area. Sometime later, he was pulled over by the police and a search of the vehicle found a satchel full of burglary tools and other restraining implements like rope and handcuffs. He was arrested for possession and other possible crimes.

Things escalated in 1975 when he was arrested for kidnapping Carol DuRonch who somehow escaped from Bundy. Bundy was convicted and received a jail sentence. Two years later, he was indicted for murder. He acted as his own lawyer. On his way to the courthouse library, he jumped out a window and escaped much to the embarrassment of the law (PCL-R #2, #5). A real Hollywood ploy?

He was captured eight days later and again he escaped through a hole he made in the ceiling. The hole was so narrow he dropped 30 pounds to snake through it. It was 15 hours before it was noticed he was missing and by then he was long gone to Tallahassee, Florida. While there, he attacked four women in the Chi Omega sorority house and killed two of them. Later he kidnapped and murdered a 12-year-old girl.

Soon he was arrested. Oddly, the mark on the body of one of the sorority girls was the exact match of Bundy's teeth where he bit the woman.

Bundy spent years on appeals for his death sentence. Psychopaths do not feel it is their fault so the appeals would be a natural reaction by Bundy (PCL-R #2, #7, #8, #16).

Bundy was so notorious, vicious, and dangerous that he became famous. He was the basis of many movies, documentaries and books. He is known for 36 killings but it is believed the total is up in the hundreds.

He ended up in the electric chair, known as "Old Sparky" at the prison. Even his death brought notoriety. While waiting for his death he still received marriage proposals from women as he did during his trial. Outside the prison, cheers and fireworks set off a party atmosphere.

As Bundy said, he read too much pornography and that caused his lifestyle. Like a true killing psychopath, he had to blame something and not himself ((PCL-R #4, #6, #8, #15, #16).

**JOHN WAYNE GACY**: total PCL-R score 32
Serial killer, sexual assaults,
Born: 1942, Chicago, Illinois.
Died 1994: Statesville Correctional Institute, Illinois.
Death by lethal injection.

Gacy had an abusive childhood and suffered from conflict over his sexuality. His father was a drunkard who beat his children with a razor strap. His mother also took some beatings. At school, he did not play with the other children. His congenital heart condition also affected his lifestyle with much inactivity (PCL-R #12).

Gacy worked as a manager of a fast food chain, became a building contractor and Democratic precinct captain for a Chicago suburb. He was "Man of the Year" by the Junior Chamber of Commerce. A picture of him with Rosalynn Carter, President Carter's wife, became famous. His life appears successful and financially well off. He was well liked in his community and was a well-known clown who performed at parties (PCL-R #1, #2, #9). He was given the nickname "Pogo the Clown" and later when his fame was known, the nickname became "The Killer Clown."

As he grew up, he realized he preferred men and boys, rather than women and girls despite being married and divorced twice (PCL-R #4, #17). He had children and stepchildren.

Gacy' lifestyle began to unravel in 1968 when he was given a 10-year prison sentence for sexual assault of two teen boys. He was released on parole after serving two years and another teen accused him of sexual assault but the teen refused to testify at the trial so charges were dropped.

A few years later two more males accused Gacy of rape and things began to turn serious with further investigations into his lifestyle (PCL-R #1, #2, #3, #5, #11, #14).

In 1974, a 15-year-old boy was last seen by his mother going to Gacy's house for a possible job (PCL-R #14). Police investigated the missing boy. A search of Gacy's house revealed that Gacy was involved in many murders, at least 33, of which were buried under the house, garage and in the nearby Des Plaines River (PCL-R #20).

In most cases, Gacy lured the victims to his home with the promise of construction work with good money (PCL-R #1, #2, #4, #5, #8, #11). He then strangled most of them with a rope, often dressed as his nickname or alter ego "Pogo the Clown."

Gacy confessed to his crimes but admitted that an alternate personality committed the crimes. Classic psychopath of not blaming himself, it was someone else (PCL-R #2, #4, #5, #6, #7, #8, #16).

He received 12 death sentences and 21 natural life sentences. He had many appeals and even denied being guilty. He had a 900 phone number set up for people to listen to his innocence. A Chicago gallery showed his paintings probably to capitalize in Gacy's fame.

Lethal injection killed him.

**JAMES WARREN JONES**: total PCL-R score 30
Mass murderer, religious or cult leader, but atheist
Born:  1931: Randolph County, Indiana, USA
Died 1978: Jonestown, Guyana

Jones's mother actually believed she had given birth to a messiah. This may have led to Jones's type of religious lifestyle. The Great Depression caused many economic difficulties and they were force to live in a hut with no plumbing. His father was believed to be connected with the Ku Klux Kan.

As a child, he was considered a weird kid obsessed with religion and death. As a child, he held funerals for dead animals and even killed some (PCL-R #2, #6, #8, #12).

At Butler University, he earned a degree in secondary education.

In 1951, he became fascinated with the Communist Party by attending meetings and rallies. The FBI questioned him and his mother about these meetings and rallies.

In 1952, he became a student pastor but he left because they would not let him integrate the blacks into the church.

So, Jones started his own church, which after many name changes became the People's Temple Christian Church Full Gospel. It was his inter-racial mission.

In time, Jones left the communist party.

In 1960, the Indianapolis mayor Charles Boswell appointed him as director to the Human Rights Commission. He was outspoken giving his views on radio and television. He gathered a following. He did a lot to promote integration (PCL-R #1, #2). He was threatened many times but some people claim he was involved in the threats for his own grandiosment. (PCL-R #5).

In order to promote his beliefs, Jones and his wife adopted many non-Caucasian children and encouraged others to do likewise. Did he adopt out of love or for promotion of his preaching (PCL-R #1, #2, #4)?

In the 1970, Jones rejected Christianity and the Bible as the Bible professed white man's justification to subordinate women and subjugate people of color. He preached he was the reincarnation of Gandhi, Father

Devine Gotama, Buda, Lenis and even Jesus (PCL-R #2, #4, #5, #7).

His move to San Francisco brought pressure onto his church so he moved to Guyana and named the town after himself, Jonestown. (PCL-R #2). The accusation from former Temple members ranged from physical abuse, emotional abuse and sexual abuse (PCL-R #11). Jones also had a drug addiction.

In 1978, Congressman Leo Ryan led a fact-finding mission to Jonestown. All hell broke out when the investigative members were at the airport to leave. Gunfire killed Ryan and five others. Later Jones convinced the members to drink the poisoned Flavor-aid (not Kool-aid) because men would now come here, torture and kill us all. Those that did not drink the flavor-aid were shot. This led to the "revolutionary suicide" of 909 inhabitants with 303 children (PCL-R #4, #5, #6, #14).

After the massacre, a report was released that stated they had found evidence of homicide, child abduction, extortion, arson, battery, drug use, diversion of welfare funds, kidnapping and sexual abuse (PCL-R #2, #3, #4, #5, #6, #7, #8, #9, #10, #11, #15, #16, #20).

**GARY LEON RIDGWAY**: total CPL-R score 30
Mass murderer, killed victims than had intercourse with dead bodies
Born: 1949: Salt Lake City, Utah
Alias: The Green River Killer

Ridgway had a troubled home life of a domineering mother with many violent arguments between his parents. His bed-wetting was a source of embarrassment to him as well as the embarrassment his mother caused with her belittling him in public and with family (PCL-R #12). As a result, he had conflicting feelings of sexual attraction and anger towards his mother (PCL-R #11).

After high school graduation, he joined the Navy and saw combat in Vietnam (PCL-R #3). His time in the military exposed him to many prostitutes. He had unprotected sex and eventually caught gonorrhea (PCL-R #11). His wife had an affair and so the marriage ended. Ridgway would have three unsuccessful marriages (PCL-R #17) but marriage did not stop his affairs with prostitutes with his love - hate relationships, which also plagued him with his mother (PCL-R #11). Ridgway almost killed his second wife with a chokehold. The chokehold became his mode of killing many of the prostitutes.

Ridgway became religious, read the Bible aloud at work and at home. He would cry after sermons, reading the Bible or other religious situations. Religion did not stop his prostitution visits or sex in public, and it created a conflict in his lust for sex and religious beliefs.

It is believed he killed 71 women but he even claimed more but he lost count. He left his victims near or in the Green River and this gave him the name Green River Killer. Strangely, after killing victims and leaving them nude in the wooded area he would return and have intercourse with the dead body (PCL-R #3, #6, #11, #14, #20).

Ridgway was arrested on charges of prostitution and as a possible suspect for the Green River killings. He passed the polygraph test which is not surprising, as psychopaths are good liars and show no emotions or empathy. The polygraph test measures emotions and it is hoped that the emotions will reveal a lie (PCL-r #1, #2, #4, #5, #6, #7, #8, #14, #20).

DNA analysis got him arrested. He plea bargained by offering assistance and was spared the death sentence for life in prison. In a grandiose sense of self-worth, Ridgway stated that murdering young women was his career (PCL-R #2, #5, #8, #15, #16).

By now one must have a feel for the traits of psychopathic killers. We can look at other killers, but we will find much of the same traits and results. When we look at these killers, we do not need tests or psychoanalysis to determine mental illness.

Ed Gein, the "Rochester killer", a psychopath killer, skinned and ate his victims. Edmund Kemper, named the "Co-ed Killer", was a sexual sadist and necrophiliac who mutilated and dismembered his victims. "The Son of Sam", David Berkowitz, found his victims in parking lots for six kills and seven wounded. Jeffrey Dahmer, the "Milwaukee Monster" tortured and killed 15 men and boys. Some killers like these were judged insane but still received maximum sentence.

Sane or not, people who commit crimes like these must be held responsible. Robert D. Hare in WITHOUT CONSCIENCE says:

> Psychopathic killers however are not mad, according to accepted legal and psychiatric standards. Their acts result not from a deranged mind but from a cold, calculating, rationality combined with a chilling inability to treat others as thinking, feeling human beings. Such morally incomprehensible behavior, exhibited by seemingly normal

people, leaves us feeling bewildered and helpless.

As disturbing as it is, we must be careful to keep some perspective here, as the majority of psychopaths manage to ply their trade without murdering people.

This is where the label psychopath is so difficult to interpret or define. Some people can score high on the PCL-R and still not be killers. Their focus is on other things like money, power, and sex, and yet the irony is that we as normal people are often attracted to the same ideals as the psychopath and fortunately, we do not kill, although at times we wish we could, but we will not. It is this refusal to kill that keeps us from the death penalty or life in jail.

Killers often have no remorse or guilt about their killing. Sometimes they even have a sense of accomplishment. Robert Hare gives an example in his book WITHOUT CONSCIOUS. A prisoner had a parole hearing coming up and the administration asked for a testing of the inmate before the hearing. Hare asked the inmate to fill him in as to why he was in the prison.

The inmate said that his girlfriend's infant daughter had been crying nonstop for hours and because she smelled he reluctantly decided to change her diapers. "She shit all over my hand and I lost my temper," he said, a grisly euphemism for what he did. "I picked her up by the feet and smashed her against the wall," he said with - unbelievably - a smile on his face. I was stunned by the casual description of his appalling behavior, and thinking of my own infant daughter, I unprofessionally kicked him out of my office and refused to see him again.

Hare later learned that he received parole a year later and was killed in a high-speed chase following a bank robbery. The prison psychiatrist diagnosed him as a killing psychopath and recommended against parole. This person was extremely glib, deceptive, conning and manipulative. He swayed the hearing in his favor for parole.

It is interesting to note how the psychopath often is able to vividly and accurately describe his killings. The details are amazing. Perhaps this means that the psychopath knows what he is doing. Perhaps a real mental problem would be someone who does not remember killing someone, as if the mind is blank at the time.

The psychopath and others like him, including women, need criminal treatment or mental illness treatment or perhaps a combination of both. Whatever, making the line between each is difficult. Psychiatrists, psychologists and law enforcers are often in conflict. After the arrest, who is in control of the situation and treatment? Is it to a mental hospital or to a prison? The difficulty in treatments is that sometimes we think the person has been cured, is released only to do crime and killing again. Sometimes they are rearrested and sometimes not. Look at Bundy and other serial killers who have been arrested, released, and kill again. It is an extremely difficult situation.

## GENENE JONES

Genene Jones was a pediatric nurse who killed 11 or 46 infants under her care. The exact number is unknown. She would inject the child with drugs to cause attacks in which she would then revive the child so that she would receive praise and attention for her work. In most cases, the child could not be revived and would die of heart failure. She was sentenced to 99 years.

"I'm a very feeling person. You can't help but fall in love with these kids," she testified. And yet, she was convicted of murdering two kids and suspected of over a dozen more. Suspicions were raised when so many deaths and near deaths where happening in her ward while she was on duty. Her commanding presence, confidence and convincing demeanor seemed to give her good cover for a while but eventually things blew up. She was good at manipulating the facts to suit her own purpose.

## BOMB DISPOSAL UNITS

A study of bomb disposal units in Northern Ireland found that such people were not psychopaths although many believed that such people had to have the psychopathic skills of no fear or guild and the love of danger. The findings were that the disposal men did not want psychopaths working with them because of their impulsiveness, unpredictability, carelessness, and undependable traits. They were loose cannons and could be dangerous. During training, the psychopaths were soon filtered out, and if they did pass, they did not last long.

In disposing of bombs, a lack of fear is not necessarily a good factor. Good bomb disposal people have a fear, often an intense fear of not being killed. It is this fear, that they control and keeps them "honest, careful, and thorough."

Stanley Rachman of Harvard University took a group of bomb disposal men who were in the business for 10 or more years. He split them into two groups: of those who were decorated for their work and those who were not. He found that once the decorated men entered the danger zone their heart rates went down as they moved into a cold meditative state.

This study is similar to a study by Fenz with parachute jumping. He studied the heart rates of experienced and non-experienced jumpers. The day before the jump and morning of the jump both groups were normal in heartbeats but as jump time approached the heart rates of both groups increased until jump time. Immediately prior to the jump, the experienced jumper's heart rates declined while the inexperienced jumpers' heart rates jumped even higher.

## PLOTTING FOR INSURANCE

Psychopaths have a feeling that nothing can go wrong because they are overly confident and grandiose in their plans. A true example of this is when a psychopath plots to kill parents or spouses for insurance or just to get rid of them. As often happens, they brag that they will soon be getting money. This bragging is a tip off that sometimes leads to police investigations. This bragging is part of the psychopath's traits that lead to their downfall.

## ROXANNE MURRAY

In 1990, on New Year's Day, Roxanne Murray killed her husband with a 12-gauge shotgun. She claimed she loved her husband but he had to die. Doug, the husband, had a need for powerful motorcycles, women and dogs. His rap sheet included many rapes and assaults, but a lack of witnesses left him free. He was married several times. He terrorized and battered his wives. Ironically, he ran a home for sexually abused teens, which gave him access to the teens for exploitation and sexual needs.

Roxanne complained about their food bill for their 14 dogs, so Doug dragged her out of the house, shot her favorite dog and told her that this could happen to you. He demanded fellatio constantly with all his women and a lack of obedience resulted in a beating. He forced women into fantasy rape scenarios. He even forced some into playing Russian roulette with a live bullet in the magazine.

The court agreed with Roxanne's action and the charges of murder were dropped.

## CLIFFORD OLSON

Here is an account of Clifford Olson, Canada's notorious killer and torturer of eleven boys and girls written in the VANCOUVER SUN by M. Farrow. What is interesting is that this article could be applied to almost all serial killers.

---

He was a braggart and a bully, a liar and a thief. He was a violent man with a hair-trigger temper. However, he could also be charming and smooth-tongued when trying to impress people... Olson was a compulsive talker... He was a real smooth talker; he has the gift of gab... He was always telling whoppers... The man was an out and out liar... He always wanted to test you to the limits... He wanted to see how far he could go before you had to stop him... He was a manipulator... Olson was a blabbermouth... We learned after a while not to believe anything he said because he told so many lies.

He talked fast, staccato... He jumped from topic to topic... He sounded glib, slick, like a con trying to prove he's tough and important.

He never showed any remorse of guilt. He would preen and pose for the camera and complained of the pictures they use of him.

## THE WAY THEY WALK

Psychologist Angel Book of Brock University in Ontario, Canada wanted to prove if Ten Bundy was right when he said that he could tell a good victim by the way she walked. She set up an experiment with undergraduate students who were rated high and low on the Self-Report Psychopathy Scale. She videotaped the gait of twelve people walking down the corridor to another room. The video was shown to the students and she found that the people who scored high on the test were better able to detect the vulnerable walkers.

She repeated the test to clinically diagnosed psychopaths in maximum security and she found the same thing in that the psychopaths could tell the best victims by the way they walked.

## JIM KOURI

Jim Kouras is vice president of the U.S. National Association of Chiefs of Police says that traits that are common among psychopathic serial killers - a grandiose sense of self-worth, persuasiveness, superficial charm, ruthlessness, lack of remorse, and the manipulation of others – these traits are also shared by politicians and world leaders: individuals running not from police, but for political office.

## GENGHIS KHAN

Let us go back in history and look at a killer, long before the word psychopath was invented. The man is

Genghis Khan. He rewrote history. He conquered the world, from Europe to the Pacific Ocean. He was brutal. He was ruthless. He earned power. He seemed to have many of the characteristics of a psychopath and yet he changed the world with many good deeds. Others have tried, like Hitler, but Genghis may well be the only one to succeed. In his book, GENGHIS KHAN AND THE MAKING OF THE MODERN WORLD, Jack Weatherford gives us many wonderful things attributed to Genghis.

Genghis Khan was a visionary leader. His conquests ranged from Europe to Asia. He brought technologies, culture, trade, inventions and ideas to all his conquered lands. He changed warfare with his new strategies and weapons for rapid attacks and siege style of war. His army was of 100,000 or less and yet his battles were against greater numbers. They won and ruled more lands in 25 years than the Romans in four hundred years. Unlike other nations at the time, the Mongols did not torture, mutilate or maim the enemy. In some cases, they were even able to get the hostages to change allegiance to Genghis.

Genghis and his Mongols may have been killers but they developed a progressive and benevolent rule. Genghis put the power of the law above his followers and himself. No one was above the law. He let his conquered people have religious freedom. He saw that public schools were developed. He awarded diplomatic immunity to officials, even if they were enemy countries at war, so negotiations could be done with no fear of death or harm. Torture was abolished.

A big accomplishment was his institution of free trade, and he created trade routes from Europe to the Far East. The trade routes opened up business and commerce as well as new foods, cultures, and ideas to all. The Mongols introduced the first paper currency and an international postal system to spread news and ideas such as printing, the cannon, the compass and the abacus. They took the local foods and moved them around the world to open up new culinary delights to all. Tea, lemons, noodles, were some of the desired foods. One of the big non-food item was playing cards, a new form of entertainment to the people.

No one in Europe had heard of China and the same was said in China of Europe but his conquests brought the two together with his trade and commerce routes. He outlawed the feudal system of advantages to aristocrats because of birth. His new system was based on merit, loyalty, and achievement. He lowered taxes for everyone and abolished taxes for doctors, teachers, priests and educational institutions. Genghis was big on education and learning new things so he pushed for a writing system.

He established a regular census. He did not believe in hoarding wealth and treasures so he distributed there goods acquired from their conquests back into commerce circulation. To keep the trade routes safe he had bandits and terrorists sought out and killed.

Genghis made stealing of animals a capital offense. People needed the animals for work and food. Anyone finding an animal had to find the owner. He developed a lost and found system for not only the animals but also for goods, money and other items. He also forbade hunting during their breeding seasons. This was a long range view to have sufficient animals during winter and future years. Animals could only be killed when necessary and not for sport or fun.

Politically, Genghis instituted laws to prevent fighting for office. Elections determined who held office. One of his laws to remove dissension in the ranks was to declare all children legitimate whether born of wife or concubine. He outlawed adultery and the selling of women into marriage and the kidnapping of women, popular at the time.

Genghis developed group responsibility with his laws. The group is responsible for the actions of the individual and the group was punished along with the individual.

With the addition of all these laws and the enforcement of these laws, Genghis ordered the adoption of a writing system to facilitate operations. He got this writing idea from the Muslims and some Christian monks who kept records. This was new to the Mongols.

> Nearly every aspect of our world - borders, political, philosophies, technologies, warfare, commerce, clothing, art, literature, language and music - bears the indelible mark of Genghis Khan and his Mongol Empire. Here is a startling true history of how one extraordinary man from a remote corner of the world created an empire that led the world into the modern age.

Geoffrey Chaucer in his CANTERBURY TALES says, "This noble king was called Genghis Khan, who in his time was of so great renown that there was nowhere in no region so excellent a lord in all things."

Genghis Khan is the classic example in the confusion of what is a psychopath is - he kills and is good to people. Some think he was just goal oriented, as killings were just the acts of war.

**REVEREND GEORGE EXOO**

From the book LOST AT SEA by Jon Ronson George Exoo was a Unitarian minister in Pittsburgh, Pennsylvania who felt he was wasting his time as his congregation was very small. One of his parishioners asked for his help as her husband had ALS, amyotrophic lateral sclerosis. His help was to help provide suicide assistance for the husband, which he did, and which in turn led to another 102 assisted suicides.

Now, the interesting aspect of these suicides is that he seems to enjoy them so much. He claims it is his calling:

> I've never done anything as important as this in my ministry. I think it is the reason I'm placed on this planet. I'm a midwife to the dying – for those who want to hasten their deaths.

One could interpret this as a grandiose sense of self-worth and a lack of guilt or remorse. Both are traits in the PCL-R test. He says he works alone like the "Lone Ranger" perhaps trying to equate himself with the doer of good deeds, a mysterious man that no one knows who he is. Exoo sets up his suicides so that the person looks like they died in their sleep. He will even prop a book up on the lap so it looks like they just died while reading a book. Like the Lone Ranger, he slips away into the sunset, having done his deed with no hanging around for congratulations and thanks.

It appears that when he goes to talk with the patient he does not try to convince them of not doing the suicide. With one client, he rushed her into the suicide, as he did not want to be hanging around in case someone came to the house. Another time, a woman did not follow his instructions, so everything was delayed and someone did come to the house. He hid in the basement until it was safe to leave. The woman did not kill herself but Exoo came back two days later to finish the job. Maybe this two-day delay may have been a good time to delay the death but he seems to want to fulfill his mission.

Exoo seems to be an actor. He is role-playing, and the thing that seems to stand out is that it appears he thoroughly enjoys his work. Is he loving the aspect of helping people or loving the aspect of killing people under the pretext of God's assistance? Should non-psychopaths enjoy the killing so much? Is he rationalizing his Lone Ranger role?

It seems that most of his patients are not terminally ill, which seems to be a very logical reason for a quick suicide too eliminate the pain. Most of his patients are suffering from depression or psychosomatic diseases.

The law catches up with Exoo. Dr. Admiral has been observing him and says that Exoo seems to enjoy the death of another person and that is dangerous. Exoo seems to have a phobia for death. In time, he became free with all charges dropped.

## ADOLF HITLER

Hitler lived before the name psychopath was developed. Was he? Probably, but was he a killing psychopath or a social psychopath. Hitler did not kill anyone through his own hands but he had many killed through his orders. Did he relish in killing the Jews like many of the German people who followed Hitler.

Germany was in devastation after WW1. Inflation and economics was almost nonexistent. He rebuilt Germany into a world power and naturally, the people would follow him. Like so many psychopaths, he did not know when to stop or ease off. He became paranoid, delusional and took on the god complex. This led to his downfall and again the destruction of Germany.

In his personality of psychopath:

He was a glib talker with charm to captivate the people. His speeches could harangue the large groups into action. It was said he could count numbers and turn the crowd into a frenzy. His philosophy for controlling the people was that it was easier to convince, control and harangue a mob, or large group, then to control and convince the individual. It worked.

He had a grandiose sense of self-worth to perhaps the god complex. He believed he was invincible.

He was good at lying and broke pacts with other countries. Lying helped get his desired results.

He was conning and manipulative, even deceitful.

He had no feelings of guilt with his killing orders and his sending of the soldiers to attack Russia where he lost an unbelievable military force. He had no feeling for the lost, just the feeling of failure to beat Russia and the deadly winter.

He was callous and lacked empathy. He could not tolerate failure by his subordinates. He was also into fits of anger and temper tantrums.

He never accepted responsibility for his own failures and inadequacies.

Hitler got off to a good start but just got carried away with his god complex. At the time he was not labeled a psychopath, as the name was not in use then but looking back at his life it is a good bet he was a psychopath.

## JOSEPH STALIN

Stalin was much like Hitler in that he personally did not kill people but he saw to it that hundreds of thousands were killed if he thought they were dangerous to his regime. The deaths were of little concern to him as he said, "One death is a tragedy; one million is a statistic."

Let us look at Stalin as a psychopath through his famous quotes. (http://www.brainyquote.com/quotes/quotes/j/josephstal136260.html#eFQSbyOOR8SCXFYS.99)

It is enough that the people know there was an election. The people who cast the votes decide nothing. The people who count the votes decide everything.

Ideas are more powerful than guns. We would not let our enemies have guns, why should we let them have ideas.

Death solves all problems - no man, no problem.

When we hang the capitalists, they will sell us the rope we use.

I trust no one, not even myself.

If the opposition disarms, well and good. If it refuses to disarm, we shall disarm it ourselves.

The only real power comes out of a long rifle.

You cannot make a revolution with silk gloves.

Gratitude is a sickness suffered by dogs.

Everyone imposes his own system as far as his army can reach.

If any foreign minister begins to defend to the death a 'peace conference,' you can be sure his government has already placed its orders for new battleships and airplanes.

Education is a weapon whose effects depend on who holds it in his hands and at whom it is aimed.

Print is the sharpest and strongest weapon of our party.

Stalin's mouth adds a little to his personality and possible psychopathic trends.

# CHAPTER THIRTEEN

# EPILOGUE

Robert Hare was interviewed by Kevin Dutton for his book THE WISDOM OF PSYCHOPATHS: WHAT SAINTS, SPIES, AND SERIAL KILLERS CAN TEACH US ABOUT SUCCESS in which he asks Hare a provocative question.

Dutton:
When you look around you at modern-day society, do you think, in general, that we are becoming more psychopathic?

Hare:
I think in general, yes, society is becoming more psychopathic. I mean, there's stuff going on nowadays that we wouldn't have seen twenty, even ten, years ago. Kids are becoming anesthetized to normal sexual behavior by early exposure to pornography on the internet. Rent-a-friend sites are getting more popular on the Web, because folks are either too busy or too techy to make real ones. And I read a report the other day that linked significant rise in the number

of all-female gangs to increasingly violent nature or modern video game culture. In fact, I think if you are looking for evidence that society is becoming more psychopathic, the recent hike in female criminality is particularly revealing. And don't even get me started on Wall Street.

Sara Konrath, of the University of Michigan may help to verify Hare's quote as she found that college students actually have a steady decline in empathy levels over the last three decades. She used fourteen thousand volunteers measured by the Interpersonal Reactivity Index. As she claims, college students are 40 percent lower in empathy than their counterparts of twenty or thirty years ago. As we have noticed, lack of empathy is a strong indicator of psychopathy.

Konrath goes even further in saying that the current group of college students, the "Generation Me," are the most self-centered, narcissistic, competitive and individualistic in recent history.

Then we have Jean Twenge of San Diego State University, who says that during this same period narcissism levels have shot through the roof. Like empathy, narcissism is also a strong trait of the psychopath.

Dutton in his book THE WISDOM OF PSYCHOPATHS tells of an email he received from a barrister - one of U.K.'s finest.

I realized from quite early on in my childhood that I saw things differently from other people, but more often than not, it's helped me in my life. Psychopathy (if that is what you want to call it) is like a medicine for modern times. If you take it in moderation, it can prove extremely beneficial. It can alleviate a lot of existential ailments that would otherwise fall victim to because our fragile psychological immune systems just aren't up to the job of protecting us. But, if you take too much of it, if you overdose on it, then there can, as is in the case with all medicines, be some rather unpleasant side effects.

Dutton also did a survey through his website. Participants answered the Levenson Self-Report Psychopathy Scale to find out their score. He also asked them their occupation and his correlation of scores with their occupation he found the following rankings.

POSITIVE
PSYCHOPATHY

NEGATIVE
PSYCHOPATHY

1. CEO                 Care Aide
2. Lawyer          Nurse
3. Media (TV/Radio)  Therapist
5. Salesperson      Craftsperson
6. Surgeon         Beautician/Stylist
7. Journalist        Charity Worker
8. Police Officer    Teacher
9. Clergy Person    Creative Artist
10. Chef            Doctor
11. Civil Servant    Accountant

# BIBLIOGRAPHY

Babiak, Paul and Hare, Robert D. SNAKES IN SUITS: WHEN PSYCHOPATHS GO TO WORK. Harper-Collins. 2006.

Burnham, Terry. & Phelan, Jay. MEAN GENES: FROM SEX TO MONEY TO FOOD, TAMING OUR PRIMAL INSTINCTS. Penguin Books. 2000.

Hare, Robert D. WITHOUT CONSCIOUS: THE DISTURBING WORLD OF PSYCHOPATHS AMONG US. The Guilford Press. New York, London. 1993.

Kevin, Dutton. SPLIT-SECOND PERSUASION: THE ANCIENT ART AND SCIENCE OF CHANGING MINDS. Houghton Mifflin Harcourt. Boston, New York. 2011.

Dutton, Kevin. THE WISDOM OF PSYCHOPATHS: WHAT SAINTS, SPIES AND SERIAL KILLERS CAN TEACH US ABOUT SUCCESS? Scientific American/ Farrar, Straus and Giroux. New York. 2012.

Greenberg, Gary. THE BOOK OF WOE: THE DSM AND THE UNMAKING OF PSYCHIATRY. Blue Rider Press. 2013.

Hodel, Steve. MOST EVIL: AVENGER, ZODIAC, AND THE FURTHER MURDERS OF DR. GEORGE HILL HODEL. Dutton. 2009.

Ronson, Jon. LOST AT SEA. Riverhead Books. 2012.

Ronson, Jon. OUT OF THE ORDINARY: TRUE TALES OF EVERYDAY CRAZINESS. The Guardian. 2006.

Ronson, Jon. THEM. Simon & Schuster. New York. 2002.

Ronson, Jon. THE PSYCHOPATH TEST: A JOURNEY THROUGH THE MADNESS INDUSTRY. Riverhead Books. New York. 2011.

Russell, Sheldon. THE INSANE TRAIN. Minotaur Books. New York. 2010

Stout, Martha. THE SOCIOPATH NEXT DOOR. Broadway Books. New York. 2005.

Theissen, Wolf. SLIP-UPS AND THE DANGEROUS MIND: SEEING THROUGH AND LIVING BEYOND THE PSYCHOPATH. Copyright 2012, Wolf Thiessen.

Thomas, M.E. CONFESSIONS OF A SOCIOPATH: A LIFE SPENT IN HIDING IN PLAIN SIGHT. Sedgwick & Jackson. 2013.

www.ingramcontent.com/pod-product-compliance
Lightning Source LLC
Chambersburg PA
CBHW060521290526
45791CB00001B/481

* 9 781515 342601 *